Life After Pet Loss

Coping With the Loss of a Beloved Companion

Lynnlee Hunt

Table of Contents

To those who feel shattered, to those who carry fragments of themselves, to those who fear they may never feel complete again after the loss of a beloved companion.

This book is for you.

May these pages offer solace in your moments of darkness; may these words be a guiding light through the labyrinth of your tired soul; may you find here a sanctuary where brokenness transforms into a pathway forward.

You are not alone in your grief journey. Together, we navigate the depths of healing, embracing the cracks as pathways to resilience and renewal.

With love and empathy,

Lynnlee

Introduction

Since you're reading this, I believe it's safe to assume that you've suffered the overwhelming sense of loss that comes from losing a pet. Perhaps you've experienced that deep emptiness and wondered why the pain feels so strong and unrelenting. You've tried to move on by distracting yourself and keeping busy, but the more you focus on other things, the more you are reminded of the absence of your beloved pet while you're following your daily routine, and the sadness and longing keep coming up.

As Anatole France said, "Until you have loved an animal, a part of your soul stays unawakened." This powerful quote captures the essence of the bond we share with our animal companions. When that bond is severed by their passing, it's perfectly natural to feel a deep sense of loss and grief that can be just as intense as losing a human loved one.

And yet, society often fails to recognize the significance of pet loss. Well-meaning friends and family may offer platitudes like "It was just a pet" or "You can always get another one," failing to grasp the depth of the connection you shared with your animal friend. This attitude leaves many people feeling isolated and misunderstood in their intense grief. And, even worse, we may even feel guilty for experiencing such intense pain and sadness.

But the grief you feel is valid and real. Your pet was a unique individual who brought joy, love, and companionship into your life. They were there for you through the ups and downs, always offering unconditional love and support. Losing them is not something you can simply "get over" or replace.

Science has begun to discover that the grief experienced after a pet loss can be just as intense as the grief felt after losing a human loved one. In fact, a 2017 study published in the journal *Animals* found that the severity of grief experienced by pet owners was comparable to that of people who had lost a spouse or child (Behler et al., 2020). In other words, grieving over your lost pet can be every bit as painful and intense as some of the worst grief imaginable.

This book is here to validate your feelings and guide you through the complex emotions of pet loss. Through these pages, you'll see that there is no "right" or "wrong" way to grieve and that everyone's journey is unique. You'll learn about the different stages of grief and how they could manifest in your own experience. But, most importantly, you'll find comfort in knowing that you are not alone. Through personal stories and expert insights, this book will provide the support and understanding you need to navigate this difficult time. That way, you can explore healthy ways to honor your pet's memory and find meaning in their loss.

You could never replace your pet. They were truly unique characters with personalities of their own, making them as impossible to replace as a child. But, as you go through this book, my hope is that you will discover hope at the end of the pain. That you will discover the ability to remember them with joy rather than sadness, and that you will be able to carry on living, always with their memory firmly in your heart.

Chapter 1:

The Animal and Human Bond

Isn't it strange how deeply an animal can crawl into our hearts? We often develop an affinity with them that we might struggle to feel for other people, which makes very little logical sense, but nobody can argue that it happens.

Then comes the terrible realization that our pets will never outlive us. The loss of our furry little companions can leave an unimaginably deep, dark void in our souls; a pain which feels as if it will never fully heal. I even know several people who feel guilty for being so sad about the loss of "just a pet."

But that isn't something to feel guilty about. When we really explore the bond between humans and their pets, we can begin to understand why they have such a profound impact on us, and why it can be so difficult to say goodbye.

Understanding the Human-Pet Bond

Many people have attempted to describe and explain the bond between humans and pets. Why are we so fascinated by these animals, and how can they become such an integral part of our lives?

According to the American Veterinary Medical Association, the human-pet bond is described as a mutually beneficial relationship that people form with animals. As we are responsible for the physical, mental, and social well-being of our pets, they become an essential part of our own mental, physical, and social well-being (AVMA, n.d.).

That's a very clinical description, isn't it? But it is accurate. Let's explore it a bit further.

Friends of mine, Jane and Tim, have been married for over 25 years. They had only one son, though they tried and failed to have a second child for many years. The couple were very close to one another, but also to their son; their small family formed a very tight bond over the years. But, as life tends to go, their son grew up and, after finishing high school, went away to college. They only saw him once every few months because he was studying in a different state.

Their home felt empty and lonely with just the two of them. Their life stagnated and, even though they loved each other dearly, they felt that they had lost a big part of their lives. It was a textbook case of empty nest syndrome.

One night, Jane was browsing through social media when she saw a photo of a puppy that was up for adoption at a local shelter. She fell in love immediately, and it didn't take long for Tim to fall in love too. Since the shelter was near his office, he went there the next day to meet the little furball and get the adoption process started.

Over the next few months, the doggy became an important member of their family. They cared for the pup as if she were a baby. She slept in their room, did everything with them, and even accompanied them on trips to visit their son. Whenever Tim brought work home, the doggy would lie on his lap and try to chase his fingers as he worked on his computer. Jane operates an online shop from home, so she constantly had a little furry companion with her as she worked.

They both say that getting a four-footed baby gave them a new reason to live. There was a new mouth to feed; a new baby to raise. And, even more importantly, she provided comfort to these two people who were suddenly very lonely.

We can't deny that the human-pet bond is very real and has a significant impact on us; in some cases more than others.

For example, there's a specific type of bond where animals help humans in a work environment. Police officers in K9 units are encouraged to form a bond with their canine partners that are as close as, if not closer than, the bond they have with human partners. It's not a matter of just having a dog that works with them. That dog is their responsibility in the same way that the dog takes responsibility for the safety of its handler (Slavik, n.d.). Even though it starts off as a work relationship, it is meant to become significantly more than that.

We can see the same bond in other work-related cases, too. Handlers who work with dolphins, whales, and other non-domestic animals can also form strong emotional bonds over time.

The bond between humans and animals evolved over several millennia. It began as a working relationship, where animals took care of physical human needs in exchange for us meeting theirs—humans provided food and shelter, while animals performed tasks. Dogs would protect, herd, or track, while cats would hunt rodents and other pests to stop the spread of disease. This symbiotic relationship gradually deepened to where we are today (Michigan State University, 2018).

In modern times, pets become members of the family. We get to know their personalities and unique characteristics. We come to love their little habits and tendencies, just like we do with our kids and other family members. Even though we can get frustrated with them at times, we can love them every bit as much as we love any human in our households.

And losing them can hurt just as much. In fact, there is no scientific difference between the grief we suffer from losing a human loved one and that of losing a beloved pet (Trepany, 2023), so we should take it just as seriously.

Scientific Studies About the Human-Pet Bond

Pet owners don't need proof of the depth of our relationships with animals. We can feel the impact of their presence and loss; in fact, we are intimately familiar with it. But because of that, people have conducted several detailed scientific studies on this phenomenon over the years, and their findings can be quite enlightening.

Pets Reduce Stress and Increase Happiness

In a study (Khalid & Dildar, 2019), researchers found what most pet owners already know: Pets make us happier!

The researchers studied the lives of several pet owners and non-owners to determine what kind of effect pets had on people. They measured stress levels and general moods in both groups over a period of time and revealed several interesting facts:

- Pet owners were generally happier and more stress-free than non-owners.

- Those who didn't have pets of their own still showed a definite improvement in their moods and a decrease in stress levels after interacting with other people's pets.

- Interacting with a pet for more than five minutes led to a drastic and immediate mood improvement and stress reduction.

- While some pet owners had dogs and others had cats, there was no significant difference between the results; in other words, it didn't matter what kind of pet it was. The presence of, and interaction with, the pet was enough to have a significant impact either way.

To summarize, the study found that pets have a definite positive impact on the mental health, general happiness, and stress-coping mechanisms of their owners.

Pets Lower Blood Pressure and Cholesterol Levels

Yes, you read that right. A study conducted in 1992 in Melbourne, on nearly 6,000 people, tried to identify if there were any significant cardiovascular health differences between pet owners and people who didn't have pets. As unlikely as it sounds, the results of the test left little doubt that pets can improve our physical health:

- Pet owners consistently had lower systolic blood pressure than non-owners. This was true of men and women, regardless of age, smoking habits, eating patterns, and socioeconomic factors.

- The triglyceride and cholesterol levels in the blood of pet owners were also considerably lower than for those who didn't have pets.

In other words, two of the common causes of heart-related health issues were drastically reduced in people who owned pets. The study also found that pet owners tended to have healthier exercise habits and live generally more active lives than non-owners (Anderson et al., 1992). But that should come as no surprise to those of us who have pets—they tend to keep us busy, don't they?

Interacting With Animals Increases Oxytocin Levels

Oxytocin is a hormone that stimulates bonding and affection. Often referred to as the "love hormone," our bodies commonly release oxytocin during bonding experiences with our loved ones. It starts when we're babies, during loving interactions with our parents, and continues throughout our lives whenever we're spending quality time with someone (Watson, 2023).

But it's not limited to human interactions. In a study published in 2012, researchers found that interactions with pets and support animals caused a dramatic spike in oxytocin levels. These results were duplicated in at least 69 additional studies, so the results are irrefutable (Beetz et al., 2012). But what does that mean for you?

- It means it is entirely possible to form a bond with an animal that's every bit as close and emotionally relevant as a bond with any human.

- Oxytocin also helps reduce our stress and anxiety levels, so there are excellent mental health benefits related to owning and interacting with pets.

- It also affects our moods. There's evidence to suggest that higher oxytocin levels counteract mental health problems like depression, though research about that is still ongoing.

- Oxytocin also plays a role in helping establish trust. As we form a bond with our pets, we begin to trust them more and more (Brennan, 2021).

The mental and physical health benefits of owning pets have been proven time and time again, and there can be no doubt that the bonds we form with our pets can be every bit as strong and loving as those we form with other people. Our pets truly become loved ones in every sense of the word. By extension, this proves that the grief and sadness we experience after losing a beloved pet can also be every bit as intense as losing any other loved one.

The Role Pets Play in Our Lives

It can be difficult to define the roles that pets play in our lives; we all just know that they do. There isn't a way to really explain it, is there? It often starts out with one practical role, but gradually increases to the point where we just can't imagine life without the furballs anymore.

The brother of a friend of mine got a dog because his wife wanted one. He wasn't really interested in getting a pet, but he agreed because his wife (who suffered from severe depression) was home alone most days and wanted companionship.

Shortly after getting the puppy, his wife tried to commit suicide by drinking a handful of pills. He got her to the hospital on time to save her life, but she was placed in a psychiatric hospital for more than a month after the failed attempt. During this time, her husband was home alone with just the puppy to keep him company. She would curl up on his lap at night as he watched TV, and they gradually formed a very strong bond. He makes no secret of the fact that his wife's puppy kept him strong through that tough time. He got the pet to help his wife feel less lonely, but his pet helped him cope with a challenging period in his life and became like a child in their home.

My neighbor, a middle-aged man whose wife had passed away a few months before I met him, went through a very dark time a few years ago. Within a two-year period, he had lost his wife, his father, and his brother. He had no family left; at least, not within driving distance. Then the COVID-19 pandemic hit, and the company he worked for was forced to shut its doors, dropping him into unemployment. He fell into a dark depression that lasted several months.

During this time, friends of his brought him a kitten. I don't approve of people giving pets as gifts, but in this case, it helped. This man suddenly had a tiny living creature that needed his care, and that gradually turned things around for him. When I spoke with him recently, he told me that he wanted to end his life several times, but every time, the thought of the kitten having to survive on her own kept him going for "just one more day." Gradually, as his bond with his cat grew, he began to feel loved and needed again, which got him out of bed every morning. He found a new job and started going out with friends. He has a new sense of purpose and new goals to live for, and he blames his kitten for the fact that he's still around today.

We can't deny that pets can help us cope with the tough times in our lives. They show us unconditional love and affection. Have you ever accidentally stepped on your pet's paw and felt that pang of guilt as they yelped and ran away? A few minutes later you are still feeling guilty, but your pet is back on your lap as if nothing ever happened. It's the very definition of unconditional love. Yes, the relationship goes both ways—we take care of them and they provide emotional comfort—but their love for us doesn't come with terms and conditions. The love of a pet is truly the purest expression of unconditional love we can find on earth.

Then we're not talking about those who have supported animals. They provide more than comfort—these pets help us overcome challenges and survive on a daily basis. Those who are blind rely on their guide dogs to take them safely where they want to go. People with less obvious conditions also rely on animals to help them cope with the circumstances of their lives, such as autism support dogs and seizure alert dogs. But we have to understand that these special requirements don't make the human-animal bond any less intense. If anything, it strengthens the bond even more.

The fact is that our pets become part of our daily lives. We arrange our schedules around them to some extent—checking their food and water, cleaning up after them, and washing them are all things we plan into our daily routines. But it's more than that. They tend to wander around wherever we are, no matter what we're doing. They'll come into the bathroom when we're taking a shower, or chase birds outside while we work in the garden. They curl up at our feet or on our laps while we watch TV, wanting nothing more than to spend every waking minute with us. This leads to frequent, consistent interactions with our pets. Some of us interact more with our animals than we do with our friends and family members.

All those small interactions throughout the day become painful memories when we no longer have them.

Why Losing a Pet Hurts So Much

So, we can clearly see that the bonds we form with our pets can become immeasurably strong, but many of us still feel it doesn't make sense for our grief over the loss of a pet to be so intense. We may even feel guilty for having such a strong sense of grief over an animal.

Carl is a young man I met a few months ago. His father passed away in 2021 after contracting a devastating virus, and the circumstances around the death of his father were traumatic to him. But his father was already deep into his 80s and, by all accounts, his health had been steadily deteriorating to the point where he was already nearly helpless when he got the virus. He was living with his daughter at the time, and she took care of him full-time. So, even though the disease was terrible to see and the circumstances around Carl's father's passing were traumatic to the whole family, they had been mentally preparing themselves for their dad's death for quite some time. This doesn't negate their grief, but they were all expecting it to happen at any moment.

A few months after his father's passing, Carl and his wife adopted a puppy from a nearby animal shelter. The pup was playful and energetic and crawled into their hearts immediately. Carl and his wife both worked from home at the time, so they had their little doggy with them most of the time.

When she was little over a year old, the puppy got sick. She didn't want to eat and would vomit all over the house. Of course, the couple immediately made plans to get her to the vet, who booked her into the animal hospital immediately; but it was already too late. Their dear puppy, who had only been with them for around a year at the time, died sometime during the night.

Carl and his wife were devastated. Everything around them felt empty. The routines they had gotten used to, like taking the doggy outside before going to bed, were suddenly pointless. That tiny living creature was no longer there with them, leaving a void that simply could not be filled with anything else.

When I spoke with Carl, he was still torn up with grief, but there was an even deeper sadness and guilt beneath the surface: he felt guilty because the grief he felt for his puppy, whom he had only known for a year, was more intense than the grief over his father's passing. Simply admitting that fact to himself, and to me, nearly broke him.

How could that even be possible? How could losing a pet hurt as much as (or, even though we don't want to admit it, perhaps *more than*) losing a loved human?

According to a 2009 study, our grief over a lost pet is directly tied to our past attachment to the pet (Field et al., 2009). In other words, the closer we were to the pet, the worse the grief. And, yes, the same is true when we lose a loved one, but because pets are such an active part of our daily lives, the level of attachment cannot be overstated. Our partners, children, friends, and other family members are important to us, but very few of them are actively there with us every second of every day. Our pets often are.

In Carl's situation, for example, he only saw his dad once every two or three weeks. He loved his dad very much, but his dad didn't play an active role in Carl's everyday existence. Furthermore, Carl had been mentally preparing for the day his father would pass away for many years because it's "normal" for children to have to bury their parents at some point.

However, the pet was a different matter. Yes, we know our pets probably won't outlive us, but we hope to have them with us for several years. And, while we have them, they are an active part of our existence to the extent that we plan our lives around them. When we want to go on holiday, there's another little creature to consider. When buying groceries, pet food is first on the list. They run around with us, play with us, and provide comfort when we need it. Then, when we lose them, not only do we miss all those things, but that same little furball we used to turn to for comfort is no longer there.

Considering these facts, it's not surprising that our grief over a pet can be every bit as intense and devastating as our grief over anyone else. Stop feeling guilty, and stop thinking about how your grief is supposed to be somehow less intense than it is. You loved that little non-human person with every fiber in your being, and they loved you back. You deserve to grieve their loss, and the grieving process will eventually help you move on with your life. So, give yourself that time and allow yourself to grieve. And, if anyone doesn't understand it, that's their problem, not yours.

In Summary

We saw that the important roles that animals play in our lives, and the bonds we form with them as a result, shouldn't be underestimated. They are more prominent than we think. It is perfectly possible for a human-animal bond to be every bit as close as the bond between two humans. Consequently, the same is true of the grief and pain we suffer when that loved one is taken away from us.

Your pet is a loved one, and you deserve to grieve for them as that, no matter what the world thinks.

The grieving process is a painful but vital step for your mental health and well-being. In the next chapter, we will explore the grieving process in more detail so you can understand what you're going through and why you're feeling the way you do.

Chapter 2:

Navigating Through the Grieving

Process

We've already seen that losing a pet is an immeasurably painful experience, but since you're reading this book, you already know that. The problem is that grief can feel like it's too much to bear, and it can be an emotional rollercoaster of sadness, deep depression, joy, and anger, all within the span of a few short minutes.

Sometimes, we wonder if it will ever end. Will things ever improve? When will we start to feel better? Is there ever going to be relief from this intense pain and hopelessness?

But this is all part of the normal grieving process, and it's important for us to go through it, no matter how painful it is.

Let's explore the grieving process. Hopefully, that will help you understand why you're feeling the way you do and find ways to cope with it.

Understanding Grief

Grief is a natural response to loss. It's not unique to humans, either; animals also suffer grief. It impacts their sleeping patterns, eating habits, and how they bond with others (Bennett, 2020). Monkeys have been known to carry the bodies of their dead babies for weeks while screaming out in grief (*The Five Animals That Grieve*, n.d.).

In other words, the pain you're feeling is completely natural and a part of one's existence. It's not a uniquely human experience, and there's nothing wrong with you for feeling the way you do. It is a deeply personal experience, and you should never compare your grief with someone else's since everyone grieves in their own way. However, there are a few typical symptoms that most people experience we will be discussing below.

The Emotional Impact of Grief

The most prominent and obvious dimension where grief reveals itself is in your emotions. You will probably experience a profound sense of sadness, loneliness, and emptiness. Everywhere you look, you will see something that reminds you of your pet, which triggers the feelings all over again.

But the loss of a pet can also trigger feelings of guilt or regret. Did you do everything possible for your beloved companion? Could you have done anything different to save their life, or make their existence happier and more comfortable?

Anger and frustration are also common. You might find yourself asking, "Why did this have to happen?" The anger might be aimed at something or someone in particular. Though there might be cases where anger can be justified, it's usually senseless when you really sit down to think about it. For example, you might be angry with the vet who didn't save your pet's life, but when you consider the circumstances, you will realize that they did everything they could.

These emotions are natural and part of the grieving process, so don't try to avoid them.

The Physical Impact of Grief

Surprisingly, grief can also have significant physical effects. It's common to experience symptoms such as fatigue, loss of appetite, difficulty sleeping, or even physical pains like headaches and stomachaches. That's because grief is a stressful experience, and the stress of losing a pet can take a toll on your body, manifesting in these physical symptoms.

It's important to recognize these signs and understand that they are probably a normal part of the grieving process, and seek medical assistance if they get too intense.

The Mental Impact of Grief

Mentally, grief can affect your ability to concentrate, make decisions, or even remember things, all of which are symptoms of a condition called "grief brain" (*Healing Your Brain after Loss: How Grief Rewires the Brain*, 2021). The overwhelming emotions you feel can lead to a sense of confusion, like a "foggy" mind. You will probably find it challenging to focus on your daily tasks or maintain your usual routines.

This mental strain is a typical response to the emotional upheaval caused by the loss of a pet, so don't be too hard on yourself.

Pet Loss Syndrome

Pet loss syndrome is a type of broken heart syndrome referring to the specific grief we experience after the death of a beloved pet. It is a type of grief which acknowledges the unique bond between humans and their pets. As we've seen in Chapter 1, scientific research on pet loss highlights that pets tend to become integral members of the family, providing unconditional love, companionship, and support. The loss of such a relationship can understandably be devastating. Pets are present in our daily lives, offering comfort and routine, and their absence can create a void that feels almost unbearable.

Pet loss syndrome is characterized by the intense sorrow and pain that comes with losing a beloved animal companion. It's important to validate these feelings and understand that they are as significant as any other form of grief (*My Dog Died and My Heart Is Broken: Hurt, Hope, and Healing*, 2010).

We have to recognize the legitimacy of grief over pet loss grief if we want to heal. Society can underestimate the severity of pet loss, but scientific studies consistently highlight that your feelings are valid and deserve acknowledgment and support.

The Stages of Grief

Apart from common symptoms, grief also typically follows certain stages, as introduced by Elisabeth Kübler-Ross in her book *On Death and Dying*, first published in 1969. Knowing about the stages will help you understand the grief you're going through and what to expect from each stage. However, keep in mind that the stages aren't clear-cut. You won't go to bed suffering from one stage and wake up with the next. They tend to overlap considerably and may repeat a bit from time to time. However, they give us a good indication of how you should progress through grief in a healthy way.

Stage 1: Denial

You've probably noticed from watching movies and TV series how people tend to react when they hear the news about someone's death—"No... No! It's not true." Perhaps you've reacted the same way or had to break the bad news to someone else who had that reaction. That's the denial stage.

The denial stage is more than that, though. It could continue for a while as you struggle to accept the truth that your pet is gone. You realize that it's the truth, and you understand it mentally, but it's as if a part of your brain doesn't want to acknowledge the fact. You act as if they are still there. The truth and finality of the situation have not yet settled in. We may even be able to tell others that our pet has passed away, so we definitely know it's real, but it does not feel real to us yet. Admitting the facts is an almost automatic process; we are simply going through the motions of letting people know.

The denial stage is a natural response—it's your brain trying to protect you from shock. We're programmed that way to protect our own sanity. However, it becomes a problem when we have trouble even admitting it. When our reality becomes so skewed that we don't even mentally believe it, it might be time to see a therapist to help us cope with the grief.

I've heard of an elderly woman who struggled with denial to the point where she kept on preparing pet meals for weeks after her cat was run over by a car. Whenever her daughter told her that her cat was dead, the grief-stricken woman would aggressively deny it and insist that her cat "was always walking around, and is probably just over at the neighbors' house." Cases like that are rare, but they happen, and counseling is usually a good idea.

Stage 2: Anger

As the denial starts to fade, it is often replaced by feelings of intense anger. The anger can be directed towards various sources, including yourself, the veterinary staff, or even your pet for leaving you. People express their anger in various ways, but it is often aimed against someone close who might have inadvertently triggered the response.

Anger is a natural response to the pain and helplessness you feel after the loss of a pet. Understand that it is normal and that it will happen, but always evaluate your anger rationally. See the situation from the other person's point of view and try to handle your anger in a healthy way.

Stage 3: Bargaining

This stage flows naturally from the anger stage. As we get angry at people or circumstances, we start to reason them out. *If only that friend had responded with the vet's details sooner. If only the vet had listened to my opinions. If only I had taken my pet to the vet the moment she stopped eating.* We bombard ourselves with scenarios in our minds of how things could have played out and how we should have done things differently.

This stage is clearly interwoven with anger, but there's also a lot of guilt and self-judgment. We can easily go down a rabbit hole of "what ifs" and "if onlys" that will only drag us down because we know that no amount of speculation could ever change the facts. That's what leads to the next stage.

Stage 4: Depression

All the reasoning, anger, and bargaining make us realize one thing: it's hopeless. There's nothing left to do. There is no injection or surgery that's going to bring them back. Praying for a miracle is not going to make one iota of a difference. They're gone, and there's nothing we can do about it. We will never see our beloved pet again.

This is a dark, depressing realization which sucks us into a void of depression and immense sadness. We feel helpless because we *are* helpless. All that's left is deep sadness, emptiness, and a sense of profound loss. We might withdraw from our usual activities and find it difficult to find joy in things we once enjoyed. Everything we do is just a process of going through the motions and looking forward to the times when the sadness lifts slightly.

Stage 5: Acceptance

Eventually, we begin to realize that life goes on. The sadness and longing don't suddenly disappear, but we gradually get back into the flow of life. We get used to the "new normal," developing new routines that don't include our pets. As time goes on, we begin to remember them with more smiles and fewer tears. It's a gradual process, but it is an indication that healing is taking place.

It's important to understand that some of us may struggle with this stage. There are cases where people feel guilty for not being so sad and depressed anymore, subconsciously thinking that they're disrespecting their pet's memory by moving on with their lives. This is not healthy. You are not forgetting about them; that could never happen. But what's better—being stuck in the pain and sadness, or remembering all the joy they brought you? Acceptance is about embracing the joyful, happy memories over the sadness of loss.

Working Through the Stages of Grief

Several years ago, the company I was working for employed a new guy. He was very friendly and talkative, and we got along well. He and his wife had both been unemployed for several months before he finally got this job, so he did his best to fit in with his colleagues and do his job well.

Only a few days after he started working there, before he got his first paycheck after being unemployed for several months, his dog got sick. He and his wife couldn't afford to take the dog to the vet, so a family friend offered to pay but they had to take the dog to the friend's vet. He happily agreed, but then had to wait a frustrating hour or two before the friend finally sent him the vet's details, and just a few hours after being booked into the animal hospital, their dog passed away.

When he got the call, his first response was that the vet was pranking him. As ridiculous as it would be, at that moment, that's what his mind told him to soften the blow. The vet was joking. He even reacted with a giggle and a "No, she's not dead. She'll be out of the hospital soon." Of course, the vet understood the grief, having had to break the news to several others over the years, and he gradually helped this grief-stricken man to understand the fact that his dog was, indeed, no longer alive.

After the call, my colleague had to break the news to his wife, which went a very similar way. She wouldn't accept the truth for several minutes before finally breaking down into tears.

For a few weeks, they were both still in denial to some extent. Though they had no doubt it happened, they instinctively tried doing the things they normally would for their pet, like getting up at certain times to take her outside or preparing her meals along with their own. They often had to remind themselves that she really was gone.

A few days after her passing, my colleague became very irritable. This friendly, joking guy would get angry for seemingly no reason. One day, I heard him venting to another colleague how he would never refer anyone to that vet because they didn't do enough. Because someone else was paying the bill, the vet wasn't willing to go the extra mile for their dog. Later I also heard him talking about how his friend had disappointed him by not sending him the vet's details quickly enough.

His irritability was directly related to the anger he felt inside, but he knew that the anger was unfair and unjustifiable. So, instead of anger, he started with a series of "if only" statements, like "If only I had gotten home sooner, I could have had her at the hospital on time." This dumped him into a pit of sadness and despair. I often walked past his desk and saw him wiping away tears. He became quiet and distant. Thankfully, most of us were supportive and didn't give him a hard time over it. Having gone through it myself, I recognized the signs of grief and remained friendly with him throughout the process.

Over time, things started to improve. He wasn't constantly sad anymore. It took several months, but he eventually even had a framed photo of the doggy on his desk, which he would look at from time to time and smile.

He made it. He had faced the pain, worked through the grief, and emerged on the other side. He still misses his pup; that will never change. But his life continues, and he has plenty of happy memories to look back on.

Coping With Each Stage

Grief is an immensely personal process, so coping mechanisms will also differ from person to person. But let's look at a few strategies you can try to find something that works for you.

Denial

- Acknowledge your feelings. Recognize that denial is a natural response to overwhelming emotions and your brain's way of protecting you from shock. Don't judge the feelings of disbelief and confusion; they are normal, so allow yourself to feel them, understanding that they will eventually pass.

- Create a new routine to help you adjust to the absence of your pet. A routine that doesn't include your pet will provide structure to keep you grounded, and it will make the loss feel more manageable over time.

- Try journaling; there's a reason why it has become so popular over the last few years. Journaling can help us express our thoughts and emotions in a clear way, which gives us a deeper understanding of why we're feeling the way we do. So, write about your feelings and experiences. It will help you process the reality of your pet's loss and help you along the path toward acceptance.

- Talk about your pet. Some of us don't want to, either because we always end up in tears, or because we don't want others to get tired of the topic. But it's important to share stories and memories of your pet with close friends or family. Talking about your pet keeps their memory alive and helps you process their absence.

Anger

- Express your anger rather than holding it in. However, it's important to find healthy outlets so you don't take it out on someone who doesn't deserve it. Options could include physical activities like running or yoga, or creative outlets like painting or writing.

- Channel your energy into positive actions and activities, like volunteering at an animal shelter or participating in community outreaches. Helping other animals (or humans) can be a way to honor your pet's memory while also making a difference in someone else's life.

- Practice mindfulness, meditation, or deep breathing exercises to help manage your anger and reduce stress. These methods have been proven to help relieve stress and complicated emotions, and mindfulness is even recommended by many anger management specialists (Tartakovsky, 2022).

- Seek support. You don't have to go through this alone. Talk to your friends, family, or even a therapist about your feelings. Sometimes just expressing your anger to a supportive listener can be incredibly healing.

Bargaining

- Give yourself a frequent reality check. Remind yourself that it's natural to have "what if" thoughts, but these thoughts don't change the reality. Acknowledge the thoughts and the emotions that come with them, but try to let them pass without dwelling on them too much.

- Focus on the positives. Reflect on the good times you shared with your pet and the love and care you provided. Celebrate the joy they brought to your life. I know, that will only increase the sadness, but that actually helps because it moves you into the next stage.

- Seek counseling. If the bargaining thoughts become overwhelming, consider seeking professional help. A counselor or therapist can help you navigate these feelings and find peace. You may feel that the death of a pet is "too trivial" to seek therapy or counseling over, but remember what we found in Chapter 1: Your grief over your pet is every bit as intense as over any other loved one.

- Join a pet loss support group. Sharing your experiences with others who understand your pain can provide comfort and help you feel less alone. You should be able to find such a group, often led by a therapist or counselor, by doing a quick web search or asking local animal shelters or therapists.

Depression

First, I want to emphasize that this does not refer to mental illness, which is classified as a disorder. In this case, we are talking about the mood or mental state of being depressed, which is completely different. People who suffer from depression are depressed even when there are no apparent reasons to feel down; people who are depressed are down because of clear and obvious reasons. The latter is the type of depression we are referring to. While the mental illness requires professional help, the mood can often be resolved without therapy and medicine.

- Allow yourself to grieve. Remember that it's okay to feel sad and to mourn your loss. Give yourself permission to experience your emotions fully. Some people even take a few days off work to grieve properly, which is an excellent idea if you are able to.

- Seek social support. Reach out to your friends, family, or support groups. Science has proven that social support plays a pivotal role in coping with loss and even reducing the chances of cardiovascular disease, which can be caused by intense grief (Czajkowski et al., 2022). Don't underestimate the value of talking to loved ones or professionals about this deep trench you find yourself in. Help your friends and family understand that you don't expect them to understand or offer advice; you just need to vent. It will make a huge difference.

- Prioritize self-care activities that promote your well-being, such as eating nutritious meals, getting regular exercise, and ensuring adequate sleep. Practice your hobbies. Do things you enjoy. Get a change of scenery. I know a woman who took an unplanned one-week road trip after her cat passed away, and it helped her mental well-being more than she ever expected it to.

- Consider seeing a therapist or counselor, especially one who specializes in grief. They can provide strategies to help you cope with depression and work through your emotions. They are trained to understand what you're going through and can help guide you through the emotional void.

- Engage in creative activities like art, music, or writing. If you're not really the artistic type, find other creative avenues to explore. These activities can be therapeutic and often provide a way to express your feelings in a unique way.

Acceptance

As the sadness becomes more bearable, you will realize that you're entering the acceptance stage. Your approach can now change a bit. Instead of trying to avoid the past, you can begin to embrace the good times you've had with your pet.

- Create a memorial to honor your pet's memory. This could be a photo album, a special place in your garden, or a donation to an animal charity in their name. A friend's son, who has autism and is very skilled with computers, designed and 3D printed a cross to place on their puppy's grave as a way to express his love for their deceased pet. So, don't be limited; embrace your creativity and express your love for them in any way you see fit.

- Celebrate their life by remembering the joy your pet brought you. Share happy memories and stories with friends and family. Create posts for social media to tell everyone how remarkable and special your furry little companion was.

- Incorporate new activities into your daily life, but make sure they bring you joy and fulfillment. This can help you move forward while keeping your pet's memory alive.

- Engage in mindfulness practices to help you stay present and focused on positive memories. As we've seen, mindfulness can help reduce anxiety and promote emotional balance.

- Help others who are grieving the loss of a pet. Your experience and empathy can be a source of comfort and support for someone else. Instead of looking for comfort from someone who never experienced what you're going through, they can find true compassion and empathy in you, so offer it freely.

Children and Grief

Even though grief is a deeply personal process, many of us have to consider family dynamics. If you're going through grief, chances are your family is going through the same process; however, they might be handling it differently, especially in the case of children.

Children experience the loss of a pet just as profoundly as adults, but their ways of understanding and expressing grief are often different. We have to understand these differences if we are to effectively help our kids navigate their grief over the death of their beloved pet.

Understanding How Children Grieve

According to the Irish Childhood Bereavement Network (n.d.), children's understanding of death and their grief responses vary significantly depending on their age, developmental stage, and previous experiences with loss.

- **Toddlers (ages 1-3):** At this age, children don't understand death as a permanent state. They might notice the absence of their pet and react to the changes in their environment and the emotions of the adults around them. Provide comfort and maintain routines to help them feel secure.

- **Preschoolers (ages 3-5):** Preschoolers may have some understanding of death but often see it as reversible. They might ask questions repeatedly and may have magical thinking, believing their pet will come back. It's crucial to offer simple, honest explanations and reassurance.

- **Elementary school children (ages 6-12):** Children in this age group begin to understand that death is permanent and universal. They may have many questions about what happens after death and can experience a range of emotions, including sadness, anger, and guilt. Encourage open communication and provide plenty of opportunities for them to express their feelings.

- **Teenagers (ages 13-18):** Teens understand death much like adults do, but they might struggle with the intensity of their emotions and the social aspects of grief. They may seek independence in their grieving process or prefer to talk with friends rather than family. Respect their need for space. but offer support and understanding when they need it.

Providing Support and Comfort

No matter how young or old your children are, it's important to offer them comfort and support. There are several ways you can do this.

- **Honest communication:** Use simple, age-appropriate language to explain what happened to the pet, but avoid euphemisms that could confuse younger children. For example, saying the pet "went to sleep" might make a child afraid of going to bed, so always be mindful of how they could interpret your explanations at their age.

- **Encourage emotional expression:** Allow your children to express their feelings in their own way. They might want to draw pictures, write stories, or talk about their pet. Validate their emotions and let them know it's okay to feel sad, angry, or confused. Tell them that you feel the same way, but that it is normal to feel those emotions.

- **Answer questions:** Be prepared for a lot of questions, especially from younger children who have never experienced grief before. Answer them honestly and patiently, even if they ask the same questions repeatedly. This helps them process the information and come to terms with the loss.

- **Maintain routines:** Keeping regular routines can provide a sense of normalcy and security for children. It helps them feel grounded during a time of emotional upheaval (and it can do the same for you).

- **Create rituals:** Involve your children in memorial activities, such as a funeral for the pet, planting a tree, or creating a scrapbook. You can help them build a memory box with various photos, pet toys, and other items that remind them of their pet. You could even let them write letters to their deceased pets to express their love and longing. These rituals can help them say goodbye and honor their pet's memory.

The Concept of "Crossing the Rainbow Bridge"

The idea of pets "Crossing the Rainbow Bridge" is a comforting concept that can help children understand and cope with the loss. The Rainbow Bridge is a fictional bridge that forms a crossing between heaven and earth. Originating in a popular poem from the 1980s, the concept suggests that pets go to a beautiful, peaceful place where they are free from pain and suffering, waiting to be reunited with their owners someday (Struck, 2021).

Parents can use this illustration to help younger kids find peace in the death of their pet. Even though it won't take the sadness away, it will help answer some questions and allay their fears and concerns.

Tips for Parents

Apart from these practical points, our children can learn a lot about dealing with grief by the way we deal with it ourselves.

- **Be a role model:** Show your child that it's okay to grieve by expressing your own emotions. Children learn by observing adults, and seeing you grieve can help them understand that their feelings are normal.

- **Listen actively:** Pay attention to your child's verbal and non-verbal cues. Sometimes, children express their grief through behavior rather than words. Be patient and listen without judgment. Offer them the same understanding that you give yourself during this difficult time.

- **Offer reassurance:** Reassure your child that the pet's death was not their fault. Just like you, your children might blame themselves for the loss, thinking they could have done something to prevent it. Be quick to explain to them that this is simply not true.

- **Read books together:** There are many children's books about pet loss that can offer comfort and help open the door for discussions. Books can offer a way for kids to explore their feelings and understand that others have gone through similar experiences.

- **Seek professional help if needed:** If your child's grief seems overwhelming or prolonged, consider seeking the help of a child psychologist or counselor who specializes in grief. They can provide additional support and strategies to help your child cope.

Resources

There are plenty of organizations that offer assistance and help to those suffering from grief in general, and some specifically for pet loss.

- **Pet Compassion Careline:** This service, based in Canada, can put you in contact with therapists to help you cope with the grief of losing your pet. It is available 24/7, and you can reach it here: www.gatewayservicesinc.com/pet-compassion-careline.

- **Everlife Memorials:** Everlife Memorials has a directory of pet loss support groups, sorted by state. Some are run by organizations like the SPCA, while others are independently operated. You can find the directory at www.everlifememorials.com/Pet-Loss-Support-Groups-s/443.htm.

- **Association for Pet Loss and Bereavement (APLB):** This non-profit organization caters to the needs of people grieving their lost pets. They let members post memorials for their pets, which can be a great way to show how much your furry companion meant to you. However, the website also offers guidance to help you through the grief period and can put you in contact with someone to talk to. You can find the APLB at https://www.aplb.org.

In Summary

Grief is a terrible thing to go through. The emotional rollercoaster and feelings of hopelessness often feel like they will continue forever. But in those times it's important to remember that it is normal to feel this way. In fact, it's evidence of how much you loved your pet and miss their presence in your life. If their passing didn't affect you like this, it means you didn't love them as passionately as you did. In some ways, grieving is the greatest compliment you can give your pet after their passing.

But that doesn't make the process any easier, does it? That's why you have to remember that it will get easier. This is a temporary emotional state, and you will get out the other side. If things get too much, reach out to someone you can talk to. You will eventually reach the end of the void, and there will be light, love, and peace.

It's also important to remember that you shouldn't hold on to the grief out of respect for your pet. Healing is essential, and that involves keeping your pet's memory close in some way. We will dive into that aspect in more detail in the next chapter.

Chapter 3:

Memorializing Your Pet

Memorializing a beloved pet is a deeply meaningful and healing part of the grieving process. A memorial allows you to honor your pet's memory, celebrate the joy they brought into your life, and find comfort during difficult times.

But how should you memorialize your pet? Since we all grieve differently, it's important to remember that there's no right or wrong way to memorialize your pet. What works beautifully for one person may be completely pointless for another. So, as we go through a few options and suggestions in this chapter, remember to adapt it to something that will be meaningful to *you* and remind you of the good times you've had with your pet.

The Science of Grief and Memorialization

We've seen how grief over the loss of a pet can be every bit as intense as grieving over any other loved one. But it's more than just an observation; it is based on science. Multiple in-depth studies have confirmed this, and it's because most people in the Western world consider their pets to be members of their family (Pirrone et al., 2015). In other words, losing your pet is like losing any other member of your close family, which makes the pain and grief every bit as intense.

But did you know that grief over a pet can last even longer? Some studies have found that, while grief over a lost loved one could last several months, it is possible for pet loss grief to last over a year (Thomas & Sours, 2007). It can also be worse than grieving a human family member because of how close we are to our pets and the unconditional love we share.

To make matters worse, pet loss grief is called a "disenfranchised grief," meaning it is not openly recognized and often downplayed by society, similar to grief over a miscarriage or a divorce (Trepany, 2023). Most companies will have no problem approving compassionate leave when we lose a spouse, parent, child, or sibling. Even attending funerals for aunts and uncles is usually no problem. But the moment we ask for compassionate leave to grieve the loss of a pet, managers are usually far less understanding.

The fact is, your grief is every bit as intense and valid as any other type of grief, and you need a healthy outlet to help you cope with it. Memorialization can help you do that.

When we lose a human loved one, certain actions are expected. Depending on your cultural background, people will immediately start asking when the funeral or memorial service will be held. It's a societal norm. In fact, during the COVID-19 pandemic, memorial services were limited or prohibited in many regions of the world, and we are now starting to see the consequences: people are suffering from prolonged grief, a recognized mental disorder (Mitima-Verloop et al., 2022).

In other words, memorialization in some form is a crucial part of our mental and emotional recovery after suffering the loss of a loved one. If the grief over a pet is just as intense, why don't we attach the same value to their memorialization? Why do people frown upon the thought of gathering a few friends and family members to celebrate that little life and mourn the loss?

Scientifically, memorialization can help us in two primary ways (*How science has proven funerals help with the grieving process*, 2023):

- It helps us accept our loss. We've seen how the denial stage of grief causes us to have trouble accepting that they are gone forever. A part of us holds on to "magical thinking"—the false belief that they will somehow be coming back (Dyring, 2022). When we plan some kind of memorial, it begins to drive home the subconscious realization that they are truly gone. In other words, memorialization helps us move past the denial stage, progressing the healing process.

- Memorialization provides stability. Planning the memorial will help focus your mind on practical things instead of dwelling on the pain. Furthermore, having some form of memorial can create new habits and routines to help in your healing.

We shouldn't underestimate the healing power of memorialization. But what is the right way to do it? That depends on you and your circumstances, but let's look at a few ideas.

Different Ways to Memorialize Your Pet

It's important to understand that memorializing your pet is a deeply personal and emotional process. You have to decide on a type of memorial that works for you; one that will truly express your love and longing for them and help you celebrate their life. So, don't feel limited by what others have done. However, if you don't know how, there are some helpful ideas that others have used.

Photo Albums and Scrapbooks

Creating a photo album or scrapbook can be a beautiful way to capture the moments you shared with your pet. These collections can include:

- **Photos:** Collect pictures from the different stages of your pet's life, starting with playful puppy or kitten days and gradually moving on to more recent moments. Add them all to the album or scrapbook, and consider adding captions or dates to remember specific events or milestones. What made those photos special? What do you remember about that day in particular? The memorial is yours, so add anything you think is relevant.

- **Mementos:** You may include items like your pet's collar, tags, or even a favorite toy. Such physical reminders can evoke powerful memories and, eventually, provide much-needed comfort.

- **Anecdotes:** Write down funny, heartwarming, or relevant stories about your pet. Think back on things they did that you found interesting or funny, then write them down in your own words. These stories can help you relive those cherished moments and celebrate your pet's unique personality.

- **Letters and notes:** You might want to include letters or notes you've written to your pet, expressing your love and the impact they had on your life.

This can be an ongoing project that you can return to throughout the grieving process. Don't be in a hurry to do it all instantly—take your time with it. It's the process that brings healing, and rushing it will only ruin the experience.

You can find scrapbooking supplies at craft stores, but there are also many online resources you can use to create digital photo books if you prefer a more modern approach. In fact, many smartphones' photo gallery apps can help you gather photos and videos together into a single album that you can use as a kind of memorial.

Paintings or Drawings

A painting or drawing of your pet is another meaningful way to keep their memory alive. Many artists can capture the essence of your pet in a way that photos sometimes cannot. If a photo isn't taken at exactly the right time, the character and personality your pet displayed in that moment is lost. Meanwhile, an artist who watches videos of your pet might be able to accurately convey that character in an artwork.

There are several options you can consider:

- **Professional artists:** Many artists specialize in pet portraits and can create lifelike representations of your pet. You can find artists by searching online, attending art fairs, or through recommendations from friends.

- **Custom art:** Some artists offer custom art pieces that can even incorporate your pet's ashes or fur into the artwork, which can be a unique and deeply personal tribute.

- **DIY art:** If you enjoy painting or drawing, you might prefer to create your own artwork, which can be therapeutic activity and a deeply personal way to honor your pet.

Planting a Tree or Creating a Garden

Trees or gardens in memory of your pet are a living tribute that grows and changes over time. It offers a way to celebrate your pet's life and create a peaceful place for reflection. There are several ways you could implement this.

- **Memorial trees:** Choose a tree that holds special meaning for you or is known for its longevity. You can usually plant the tree in your yard, or use a designated memorial space—some communities offer areas specifically for this purpose.

- **Garden spaces:** Design a garden with flowers, plants, and decorations that remind you of your pet. These could be anything they particularly enjoyed, like plants they loved playing around in. You can even include a small plaque or marker with your pet's name and a special message to indicate that this is a dedicated garden area.

- **Dedication plaques:** If it isn't possible for you to plant a tree or create a garden in your own space, look for local parks or community gardens that offer tree planting or bench dedication programs in memory of loved ones, including pets. Create a plaque and place it in this area to honor their memory.

Memorial Services

A memorial service can be a healing ritual. It gives you an opportunity to gather friends and family members to honor your pet's memory.

Remember that a memorial service doesn't have to be an impressive event or occasion. You don't have to book a church or hall. A small, intimate gathering in your living room or garden can be just as effective, and possibly even more heartfelt since you will be in an area your pet was familiar with. So, choose a location that was significant to you and your pet, such as your home, a favorite park, or the backyard.

Invite close friends and family who knew your pet and can offer support. You can also invite fellow pet owners who understand the depth of your loss. Select poems, readings, or songs that were meaningful to you and your pet. These can include pieces specifically about pets or general themes of love and loss.

Encourage attendees to share their favorite memories and stories about your pet. This can be a comforting way to remember the happy times and the joy your pet brought to everyone's lives. You may also want to consider including a symbolic act, such as lighting candles, releasing balloons, or planting a flower. You may want to scatter ashes or, if it's a burial, you could do that during this time. These rituals usually provide a sense of closure and peace.

Keepsake Boxes

A keepsake box is similar to a scrapbook or album, but it is more dynamic. For example, it's often difficult to add larger items like toys or collars to a scrapbook. A keepsake box makes it easy to include anything you want, such as photos (perhaps in an album or scrapbook), collars, tags, blankets, and favorite toys. You can also add a lock of their fur, if you have it.

The great thing about a keepsake box is that you can add more items to it as time goes on. There's usually a period after the passing of a pet that we often discover more items they've left behind, like a ball hidden under the bed, or a chew toy buried in the couch. As you discover these items, you can add them to the keepsake box. If you write letters, notes, or poems about your pet, you can also include them.

Digital Tributes

The digital age offers many new ways to create online or electronic memorials for your pet.

- **Social media posts:** Share a tribute post on your social media accounts, including photos and stories. This allows friends and family to offer their condolences and share their own memories.

- **Memorial websites:** Create a dedicated memorial website or blog where you can post photos, videos, and written memoirs of your pet. Websites like ForeverMissed or Rainbow Bridge offer platforms for creating lasting digital tributes. Writing on these platforms can help you gather your thoughts and clear your mind, allowing you to work through your grief more effectively.

- **Digital photo galleries:** As mentioned, most smartphones' photo gallery apps have excellent album-making capabilities. Many of them can even automatically compile sets of photos and turn them into a slideshow, often with music, that you can save to your device, watch whenever you want, and even share with others.

- **Virtual memorial services:** If friends and family are spread out geographically, consider hosting a virtual memorial service using online streaming tools like Zoom. This allows everyone to participate and share their memories, no matter where they are.

Personalized Memorial Items

Many companies offer personalized items to help you remember your pet. There's virtually no limit to the options available, and new ideas seem to come up daily, but some popular choices include:

- **Custom engraved stones:** Some companies can create a custom engraved stone with your pet's name, dates, and a special message. These stones can be placed in your garden or a favorite outdoor spot.

- **Memorial plaques:** You can display personalized plaques in your home or at a favorite location to provide a lasting tribute.

- **Photo blankets and pillows:** Some companies offer services to print your pet's photo on blankets, pillows, and other items, allowing you to keep a physical reminder of your pet close.

Keep in mind that memorialization is personal. Use these ideas, but be creative in how you implement them. If you want to change some aspect of any idea, that is up to you. You're the one who knew your pet best, so memorialize them in any way you see fit.

Keeping Your Pet Close

Most of us find comfort in keeping some physical aspect of our pets close after their passing. We do this in several ways, depending on the circumstances. Some find certain aspects uncomfortable, so it's vital for you to choose a way that works for you.

Let's explore some options for preserving your pet's remains and creating lasting keepsakes that allow you to feel a continued connection with your furry friend.

There are essentially two options we can choose after our pets pass away: cremation and burial.

Cremation

Cremation is becoming an increasingly popular option because it offers lots of flexibility. You have the option to scatter the ashes in a place that's meaningful to you and your pet, but you can also carry the ashes with you in various ways to always feel like you have them close. Cremation truly offers us plenty of ways to memorialize our pets. Let's look at some popular options.

Urns

An urn is a popular way to keep your pet's ashes close. You can display the urn somewhere in your home, and if you move to a new home, you can take the ashes with you, which is not something you can do if you choose burial.

Pet urns come in various styles and are made of a variety of different materials, including wood, metal, ceramic, and biodegradable options. You can choose an urn that reflects your pet's personality or your home's decor, making it easy to create a special place to honor your pet.

Urns can be kept in a prominent place in your home to serve as a daily reminder of your pet's presence.

Memorial Jewelry

It's possible to incorporate your pet's ashes into jewelry, offering a unique way to keep them close to you at all times. Memorial jewelry options include pendants, rings, bracelets, and even earrings.

Companies like Parting Stone offer innovative services that turn your pet's ashes into 40 to 60 small, solidified cremation stones. You can carry these stones in your pocket, place them in a special location, or share them among family members. You can find Parting Stone online at partingstone.com.

Keepsake Items

Beyond jewelry, there are also other keepsake items where you can incorporate ashes. These include keychains, glass sculptures, or even custom-made art pieces where the artists include the ashes in their paint when painting a portrait of your pet. These items offer a tangible connection to your pet and can be a comforting presence in your daily life.

Burial Options

Burial is the more traditional option of the two. Even though it is falling out of popularity, it is still a viable option in many cases. While cremation offers you the flexibility to keep your pet's remains close, burial offers the opportunity to create a memorial where you can celebrate your pet's life.

There are two basic options when it comes to burial: a home garden or a pet cemetery.

A Home Garden

Burying your pet in your home garden can create a personal and accessible memorial site. You can bury your pet in an area that meant a lot to them (and you).

This site can be a comforting place to visit and reflect on all the good times you had with them. You might consider planting flowers, shrubs, or a tree over the burial site to create a living tribute, or you can also add a small plaque or marker with your pet's name and a special message to designate the spot. Because it's your space, you can make the memorial site as simple or elaborate as you like.

Pet Cemeteries

Many cities and towns now offer pet cemeteries specifically to bury pets. They offer a formal place for burial, similar to human cemeteries, with a dedicated and maintained space for you to visit. Some of these cemeteries provide additional services, such as gravestones, plaques, and perpetual care. Several pet cemeteries even offer memorial walls to place your pet's ashes if you choose to cremate them.

Choosing a pet cemetery can offer peace of mind, knowing that your pet's resting place will be cared for in the long term. It is also a viable option if you don't own a home, might move at some point, or don't have a garden where you live. But keep in mind that pet cemeteries usually have rules and guidelines regarding business hours and the type of memorials you're allowed to add to graves.

Personalized Memorial Items

Apart from what you do with their actual remains, remember there are also other ways to memorialize your pet and keep some reminder of them close. Some options include:

- **Custom engraved stones:** You can get memorial stones engraved with your pet's name, dates, and a special message or quote. These stones can be placed in your garden, a favorite outdoor spot, or even indoors as a decorative piece.

- **Photo memorials:** You can order or print custom photo items, such as blankets, pillows, or framed prints, that feature your favorite images of your pet. They allow you to keep a visual reminder of your pet in your home and can be particularly comforting in the early stages of grief.

- **Keepsake boxes:** We already discussed keepsake boxes, but it's worth emphasizing that a keepsake box is an excellent way to keep some physical element of your pet close to you as you work through the grief.

Memorializing Through Actions

In addition to physical mementos, you might want to consider actions that honor your pet's memory and keep their spirit close.

- **Charitable donations:** Making a donation in your pet's name to an animal charity or shelter can be a meaningful way to honor their memory. If you adopted your pet from a shelter, making a donation to that shelter is a great option. This act of kindness can help other animals in need and create a lasting legacy for your pet.

- **Volunteering:** If you can, volunteering at an animal shelter or rescue organization can be a therapeutic way to cope with your loss while honoring your pet's memory. It provides a sense of purpose and connection while keeping your pet's spirit alive through your actions.

- **Creating a memorial fund:** A memorial fund in your pet's name can help you support causes that were important to you and your pet. This could be a fund to help with veterinary care for animals in need, support for pet adoption programs, or any other animal-related cause.

In other words, you don't have to be limited by what others have done. If something is meaningful to you, and you feel it's a good way to honor your pet's memory, that is worth doing. Memorializing through actions can help turn your loss into someone else's gain, possibly keeping someone else from experiencing the pain you're feeling right now.

Personal Stories

To give you some ideas, let's look at a few creative ways that people have memorialized their pets.

Jane and Twinkie

Jane is a stay-at-home mom who takes full-time care of her son. During the day, while her husband was at work, Jane would often get a bit lonely and bored, so she and her husband decided to adopt a puppy from a local animal shelter. They named her Twinkie, and both of them immediately fell in love with the tiny fur ball. She was a lively and cheerful presence in their home.

After about 18 months, it became apparent that Twinkie wasn't well. Jane rushed her to the vet, who gave her medicine and sent them home. When Twinkie didn't get better after two days, Jane took her back to the vet, who told Jane that he would have to keep Twinkie overnight. That night, Twinkie passed away.

The family was heartbroken. Even after such a short time, Twinkie had become a huge part of their family, and everyone missed her. But they had a choice to make and very little time to do so: what would they do with Twinkie's remains? Being unable to afford cremation at the time, they fetched their puppy's tiny body from the vet and took her home one last time to bury her in the garden. They held a small ceremony with a few friends who also adored Twinkie, after which Jane visited the grave several times each day for many months.

But there was another challenge: her husband's job required them to relocate to a different town a few months later. This was a significant problem because they knew they had to leave their pet behind and only had her toys to take with them.

That's when Jane had a brilliant idea. Knowing how much Twinkie loved strange scents, like lavender, she bought two lavender plants and planted them next to Twinkie's grave with a small engraved stone. When they moved a few months later, Jane replanted the lavenders in pots and took them, with the stone, to their new home, where she created a new memorial in their garden. It wasn't an ideal solution, but it gave the family some comfort as they continued down the path of grief and healing.

Carl and Poppy

Carl is a middle-aged man who went through an ugly divorce a few years ago. After the divorce, he threw himself into his career and, in his depression, he didn't really get out much. He neglected his friends and family because he didn't have the energy for social interaction.

Realizing that he was lonely, and in an attempt to change his life a bit, he adopted Poppy when she was just a tiny little kitten. Poppy brought life into his home and gave him a sense of purpose beyond his job.

Over the next few years, he gradually rediscovered his will to live, and he praises Poppy for giving him that.

When she was three years old, Carl discovered that Poppy had a lump in her stomach. He took her to the vet, who discovered that the cat had cancer, and it was already in the advanced stages. There was very little they could do for her, and eventually, Poppy had to be euthanized to relieve her of her pain and suffering.

This destroyed Carl and almost dropped him back in depression. If not for the friends he'd made over the last few years, he probably would have. But this caused Carl to make a drastic decision: he would stop smoking.

He had been a heavy smoker for more than 15 years at the time. Even though he had tried to quit several times, he would always cave to the cravings after a few weeks. When Poppy died, he made the decision that every breath he took would be a memorial to Poppy who, in many ways, had saved his life. He made that decision more than five years ago, and he hasn't smoked a single cigarette since then, and he never passes up an opportunity to tell others about his remarkable cat who saved his life in more ways than one.

Kim and Lula

Kim was 15 years old when she got a puppy called Lula. The pup became Kim's constant companion as she worked her way through High School and, eventually, college. When Kim got married at age 24, Lula moved into her new home and was a member of the family. They shared a bond that, in Kim's own words, was unlike any other bond she had ever experienced.

Lula lived to the ripe old age of 12 before she eventually passed away. Kim knew that her pet was getting old, so she had been mentally preparing herself for the sad day for a long time, but when it happened, she was still struck with grief when the reality of Lula's passing hit home.

Kim wanted to memorialize Lula in every possible way. She got Lula's ashes in a beautiful urn and displayed them on a shelf with photos of other departed loved ones, accompanied by a photo and one of Lula's favorite toys. She also ordered a silver bracelet and a gold ring, both engraved with Lula's name, to carry with her every day. Since Lula always loved to play around in the flower garden, Kim placed fresh flowers next to her ashes once a week to pay tribute to her memory.

Even though it happened several years ago, Kim still honors her pet in this way, and Lula still has a place of honor in their home.

In Summary

Memorialization is a proven way to help comfort us through the grieving process. It can help us come to terms with the passing of our pets and move past the denial stage. It also provides a sense of comfort, since we can feel close to our pets, even though they are no longer there.

When the grief is still raw, it's easy to think we don't want to face the reality by dealing with their remains or creating a memorial. Some of us just want to avoid the topic entirely. But this is not healthy and will only extend the grieving period. We have to face those emotions and work through the process to get healing and remember the good times with our pets, and memorialization plays an important role in that.

How you memorialize your pet is up to you, but it's important to do it. Even if you just write them a letter to tell them how much you miss them, or create a keepsake box or scrapbook, it's vital for your mental health to have something tangible that can help you work through the pain you feel and guide you through the void.

Chapter 4:

Pet Loss Support Groups

We humans can be strange sometimes. When we're sick, we might try to treat the problem ourselves for a while, but when things don't get better, we usually won't hesitate to see a doctor. So, why are we so hesitant to do the same for our mental health?

We are gradually beginning to realize that our mental well-being is every bit as important as our physical health. In fact, mental and emotional problems often manifest in our bodies and cause a variety of problems. Scientific studies confirm this, as we'll see in a moment. And yet, many people still believe that going to therapy or attending a support group is a sign of weakness.

There's no doubt that you are going through a lot right now. Some days may be okay, but the sadness and darkness can overwhelm you at any minute. We've seen how badly the loss of a pet can affect us, but we can make life so much easier for ourselves when we're willing to reach out to someone. Family and friends can fill that gap to some extent, but they aren't necessarily the right people to help us, especially in cases where the struggle becomes too much. For those times, we have two excellent options: support groups and counseling services.

Support groups can be great because you can talk to others who know exactly what you're going through. They understand your situation because they've been there, so they can offer guidance and tips that helped them. Counseling services, on the other hand, put you in contact with someone who's trained and experienced in helping people cope with (and overcome) the pain and challenges of grief.

Let's look at both options in more detail.

Understanding Support Groups

Support groups are often overlooked, but they can play a pivotal role in helping us cope with the loss of a pet. These groups provide a space where we can share our experiences, express our emotions, and receive support from others who understand what we are going through. As we grow and work through our grief with the help of others, we will eventually get to the point where we can help others by sharing what we went through and how we coped. It's a perfect symbiosis of people helping each other through their waves of grief.

Unfortunately, not all support groups are equal. Some might simply not be the right fit for you, while others lack proper guidance and could become unhealthy environments. So, before you decide if this is the right option for you, let's look at what a support group is, how it should function, and how it can help you with your struggle.

What Is a Support Group?

A support group is essentially a group of people who come together to share and discuss common experiences or concerns. Perhaps the most famous example of a support group is Alcoholics Anonymous (AA), but there are support groups for just about any type of emotional or mental struggle.

In the context of pet loss specifically, support groups consist of people who have lost a pet and are seeking comfort, guidance, and understanding from others who have had the same experience and feelings. The groups can be organized in various formats, including in-person meetings, online forums, or virtual video calls.

How Do Support Groups Function?

Support groups usually function under the guidance of a facilitator, who may be a professional counselor, a trained volunteer, or a group member with experience in leading discussions. It is the facilitator's role to ensure that the conversation flows smoothly, that everyone has the opportunity to speak, and that the group remains a safe and supportive environment. Because all the people attending the meeting are going through emotional struggles, and everyone deals with their feelings in different ways, things can quickly get heated, unfair, or off-topic if there isn't someone who can lead the discussion and help keep people's feelings in check.

During meetings, group members are encouraged to share their stories, talk about their feelings, and offer support to one another. This mutual exchange can include discussing memories of their pets, the challenges they face during the grieving process, and the ways they are coping with their loss. Some groups may also incorporate activities such as reading and discussing articles or books about pet loss, participating in memorial activities, or engaging in relaxation techniques and stress management exercises.

Why Are Support Groups Useful?

Support groups offer several benefits, mainly because they provide social support, which is crucial during times of grief. Remember that those who attend groups are all at different stages of the grieving process, so someone who is in the anger stage can benefit from the wisdom of another person who is already entering the acceptance stage.

This social support can take on different forms, depending on what we need at the time.

Emotional Support

One of the primary benefits of support groups is the emotional support they offer. When grieving the loss of a pet, we could occasionally feel isolated, misunderstood, or overwhelmed by our emotions. In a support group, we can find a community of people who genuinely understand our pain and can offer empathy and encouragement. This sense of belonging can be incredibly comforting and help alleviate feelings of loneliness. In fact, since everyone is facing the same struggles, it's not uncommon for people to make friends with other members. Those friendships can blossom into some of the most caring and supportive relationships in our lives.

Informational Support

Support groups usually provide informational support by sharing knowledge and coping strategies. This could come from the facilitator, especially if they are a trained therapist or counselor. However, group members can also exchange practical advice on dealing with grief, such as ways to memorialize a pet, how to handle well-meaning but insensitive comments from others or tips for maintaining a daily routine while grieving. The collective wisdom shared by the group can be invaluable, especially for those who may be experiencing the grief of pet loss for the first time.

Practical Support

In some cases, support groups may also offer practical support, such as helping members connect with additional resources, like pet loss counselors or grief workshops. Facilitators or group members may have knowledge of local services and organizations that can provide further assistance. Some people find comfort when other members attend their memorialization activities. It all adds to the sense of community and mutual understanding.

The Positive Impact of Social Support

Scientific research is consistently showing the positive impact of social support on people's mental and emotional well-being.

For example, a study published in the Journal of Vocational Behavior found that social support helps people cope with emotional stress on three different levels (Viswesvaran et al., 1999):

- It reduces the amount of strain people experience.

- It lowers the emotional impact of aspects that cause stress and emotional strain.

- It mitigates the relationship between stress and strain.

While this study mainly focuses on work-related stress, it also found that the same principles apply to other forms of stress, including the grief we experience after losing a pet.

In other words, social support buffers the negative effects of stress by providing a sense of stability, security, and belonging. It can help us reframe our experiences in a more positive light, reduce the feelings of helplessness we experience, and enhance our ability to cope with difficult situations. As you struggle through the pain of losing your pet, having a supportive community can make a significant difference in helping you work through the grieving process by helping you feel understood and less alone in your sorrow.

The Healing Power of Shared Experiences

One of the most powerful aspects of support groups is the healing that comes from shared experiences. When we share our stories and listen to those of others, we often find that our feelings and experiences are mirrored in those of the other members. This validates our feelings and experiences, which can be a crucial step in the healing process since it reassures us that our grief is real, normal, and worthy of attention.

Hearing how others have navigated their grief can also provide hope and inspiration. It demonstrates that, while the pain of losing a pet is profound, it is possible to find a path forward and integrate the loss into our lives in a meaningful way.

Types of Support Groups

Support groups come in various forms, and it's up to you to decide which type will work best for you. They all have their pros and cons, but all types are useful.

Online Forums

Online forums are virtual communities where individuals can post messages, share their experiences, and offer support to others, usually through text chats. These forums are accessible 24/7, so they offer a convenient option for people with busy schedules or those who prefer the flexibility of participating from the comfort of their own homes.

Benefits of Online Forums

People might think that an online forum isn't a "real" support group, but that is not the case. It is possible to connect with others and reap all the benefits of a support group through these platforms, but they offer other benefits, too:

- **Anonymity:** Online forums often allow users to remain anonymous, which can make it easier to share personal feelings and experiences without fear of judgment. It's easier to say what's really on your mind when you're not seeing other people face-to-face.

- **Accessibility:** Anyone with internet access can participate in online forums from anywhere in the world, at any time. This makes them a great option for those who live in remote areas or have limited mobility.

- **Diverse perspectives:** Online forums often attract a wide range of participants from different backgrounds and locations. This diversity can provide a broader perspective on pet loss and reveal different and unique coping strategies.

- **Association for Pet Loss and Bereavement (APLB):** We mentioned the APLB in a previous chapter as an excellent resource to help us through the grief of pet loss. One of its services is an online chat room (available to members only) where people can share their experiences and receive support from trained facilitators and other members. You can access it at www.aplb.org/chat-room/.

- **Rainbows Bridge Pet Loss Grief Support Website:** This website features a forum where users can post messages, share stories, and offer support to one another. It's a less interactive way to offer each other support, and facilitators and trained counselors also actively participate in the discussions. You can find the forum at forums.rainbowsbridge.com/?forum=150830.

- **Reddit:** Reddit is a social network where people can join forums (called "subreddits") dedicated to topics that interest them. You can create a free account and make it as anonymous as you like, then join one of the multiple subreddits dedicated to pet loss grief. People love sharing their experiences after losing their pets and offer each other encouragement and support. Reddit is available on the web at reddit.com or by downloading the Reddit app on your smartphone.

Sarah, an old friend of mine, lost her cat a few years ago. She was devastated since her kitty was her constant companion. The problem was that Sarah was very isolated. She had only recently moved to a new town and started a new job, so she didn't know many people. Her family and friends all lived far away. So, Sarah withdrew in her grief and didn't really reach out to the people in her small town.

After struggling on her own for several months, Sarah discovered a pet support group on Reddit. Not really one for social interaction, she browsed the group and saw what others were posting and commenting. Many of the posts resonated with her, so she eventually got the courage to post her own story. It was a short but heartfelt post, so she didn't expect much feedback, but she was overwhelmed with support from others who had been through the same struggles. They freely offered comfort and advice that helped carry Sarah through the grief.

Local Community Meetings

Local community meetings are the most well-known and recognized type of support groups. They provide an opportunity for face-to-face interaction, which can be particularly comforting for many people. The meetings are often organized by local animal shelters, veterinary clinics, or pet loss organizations, so you should be able to find one near you through a quick online search or by reaching out to your local organizations.

Benefits of Local Community Meetings

- **Personal connection:** Meeting in person allows us to form more personal connections and offers the opportunity to form meaningful relationships with others who understand our grief.

- **Structured support:** Unlike online forums, in-person meetings are usually facilitated by trained and experienced professionals or volunteers who can guide the discussion to ensure a supportive environment.

- **Local resources:** Attending local meetings can help you connect with other resources in your community, such as counseling services, memorial events, and educational workshops about coping with grief.

Examples of Local Community Meetings

- **Support groups at veterinary clinics:** Many veterinary clinics offer support groups for pet loss. They provide a familiar and trusted environment for grieving pet owners.

- **Animal shelter support groups**: Local animal shelters often host support groups to help pet owners cope with their loss and connect with others in the community.

I met Jeremy and Vanessa through an in-person group support session in my area. Their dog had only passed away a few days before, and the vet advised them to attend the group sessions. They were still struggling through the denial stage.

During the first few hours, they didn't say much. When they tried, they were overwhelmed with tears and couldn't get the words out. Until one of the other attendees spoke about how the reality of his dog's death had hit him a few weeks earlier. That triggered a response, and Jeremy started lashing out in anger. "Why did this happen? Couldn't the vet have stopped it? Why didn't he do something sooner?"

One sentence from a member of the support group triggered a raging torrent and helped Jeremy progress from the denial stage to the anger stage. That might not seem like a good thing, but remember that grief is a process—you have to pass through all of the stages to get healing, and the group brought Jeremy one step closer to that goal.

Virtual Video Conferences

Few of us are strangers to video conferences after the COVID-19 pandemic, and the world has opened up to new ways of doing everyday things, including the hosting of support groups.

Virtual video conferences combine the benefits of online forums and local community meetings in a unique way by offering face-to-face interaction through digital platforms. These meetings are typically held on platforms like Zoom, Google Meet, or Skype, and provide a convenient way to connect with others from the comfort of your own home.

Benefits of Virtual Video Conferences

- **Face-to-face interaction:** Seeing and hearing others can create a stronger sense of connection and empathy compared to text-based communication. Everyone's emotions are clearly visible, so it's easier to have empathy and offer sincere support.

- **Convenience:** You can participate in virtual meetings from anywhere if you have an internet connection and compatible devices, so they are accessible and flexible.

- **Structured environment:** Text-based online forums are often unregulated, which could lead to conflict and misunderstandings, especially because of the anonymity on many platforms. That's not the case with video conference meetings since they are usually facilitated by a professional or trained volunteer, just like in-person meetings. This ensures a supportive and organized discussion.

Examples of Virtual Video Conferences

- **Online pet loss support groups by APLB:** This is yet another great service that APLB offers to its members. The organization hosts virtual support group meetings that are facilitated by trained and experienced volunteers. These meetings provide a safe space for sharing and healing. You can find more information at www.aplb.org/online-video-support-about/.

- **Anti Cruelty's online support groups:** Anti Cruelty is a well-known animal welfare organization and shelter. Among the myriad of services they offer, Anti Cruelty also hosts regular video support groups. Unlike APLB, these sessions are open to everyone, not just members. You can find the schedule at anticruelty.org/events/virtual-pet-loss-support-group.

Understanding Counseling Services

As we've seen, the support of friends, family, and support groups can be invaluable as we're struggling through the grief of pet loss. However, sometimes the grief can get overwhelming, making us feel hopeless and helpless. In these cases not even talking to our best friends will help. That's when we might need a professional person to help us navigate complex emotions.

While support groups are amazing, counseling services offer specialized and personalized assistance from trained professionals who can offer strategies to help you work through your grief.

What Is Counseling?

Counseling is a term used to describe various types of therapy, including psychotherapy. It usually involves meeting with a trained mental health professional to discuss and address any emotional, psychological, or behavioral issues people might have.

In the specific context of pet loss, grief counseling is a specialized form of therapy that focuses on helping individuals cope with the intense emotions and challenges that come with losing a beloved pet. Grief counselors are trained to provide a safe, non-judgmental space where you can express your feelings, explore your grief, and develop coping strategies. They can help you understand the grieving process while encouraging you to work through the complex emotions you're experiencing. A grief counselor will also help you find ways to honor and remember your pet while moving toward your emotional healing.

Counseling offers several benefits, including:

- **Emotional support:** Counselors provide a compassionate and empathetic space where you can openly discuss your feelings without fear of judgment. They are trained to expect even the most severe emotions and will never judge you for expressing them. On the contrary, they encourage the honest expression of emotions. Furthermore, they offer full confidentiality, so you can even vent your anger without affecting anyone in a negative way.

- **Guidance and insight:** Counseling will help you gain a deeper understanding of your grief. The counselor will explain the reasons why you feel and react the way you do, and then help you discover healthy ways to cope with those emotions.

- **Personalized strategies:** Your friends and family, and even support groups, will offer guidance and support, but it will often be generic. "This worked for me; maybe it will help you, too." But counselors will consider your specific scenario to offer you specific, personalized strategies to cope with your struggles. In other words, you are more likely to get advice that will work in your specific situation.

- **Stress reduction:** Engaging in counseling can help reduce the stress and anxiety you suffer as a result of your grief, which promotes your overall well-being. We'll look at that more closely in a moment.

- **Validation:** Counselors can validate your feelings and experiences by confirming that they are normal and you have a right to feel the way you do. This helps you realize that your grief is legitimate and important.

- **Avoiding future problems:** Counselors may specialize in grief counseling, but they are trained to notice other problems too. Because of that, a counselor will be able to notice when you are at risk of other problems, such as clinical depression or prolonged grief. They can then intervene and ensure you get the help you need.

Grief Counseling Techniques

Counselors and therapists use various techniques in grief counseling (Bradley University, 2014). Let's look at some of these techniques.

Cognitive Behavioral Therapy (CBT)

CBT is a type of therapy that aims to identify and change negative thought patterns and behaviors. Its foundation is the belief that our thoughts, feelings, and behaviors are all interconnected; for example, our emotions influence our thoughts, and those thoughts are responsible for our actions. By changing our negative thoughts, we can directly affect our emotions and behaviors.

Through CBT, we who are grieving over the loss of a beloved pet can:

- **Identify our negative thoughts:** Recognize and challenge unhelpful thoughts, such as guilt, regret, or irrational beliefs about the loss of the pet. In other words, this helps us navigate through the denial, anger, and bargaining stages of grief.

- **Develop healthy coping mechanisms:** We can learn strategies to manage and reduce the symptoms of grief. These techniques include relaxation exercises, journaling, or engaging in meaningful activities. In the process, we learn to navigate the depression stage in a healthy way.

- **Reframe experiences:** We learn to shift our perspectives to find more balanced and positive ways of thinking about our pets and their loss. This helps us move through the depression stage and into acceptance, where we can remember the happy times we've shared with our pets.

- **Build resilience:** CBT strengthens our emotional resilience and helps us develop skills to handle future challenges. It ensures that, when we suffer grief again, we can cope with it more easily.

Acceptance and Commitment Therapy (ACT)

The basis of ACT is to help us move past our grief by embracing it in a mindful way rather than fighting it. In other words, instead of trying to resist the grief or holding it back, we accept that we are grieving and learn to observe the grief as a neutral reality, removing all passionate responses from it. It is strongly formed around the basis of mindfulness practices, which are actions we take to be present in each moment.

ACT teaches us six different tools we can use to overcome grief:

- We learn to focus on our own values and the things in life that are most important to us.

- We commit to taking action and achieving goals. In other words, we start focusing on doing things in our lives rather than wallowing in depression.

- We learn to accept that we are experiencing difficult emotions, but without judging them. There are no good or bad emotions—there are only emotions. They are there, we accept them as real, but we recognize that they are part of the process and aren't inherently bad.

- We strive to become more aware of our daily activities and consciously invest time and energy into them.

- We learn to create space between ourselves and our thoughts; a process known as cognitive defusion. In other words, we recognize that our thoughts don't define who we are and don't demand justification or action.

- We develop the "observing self"—a way of viewing ourselves as separate from our thoughts and emotions. So, even though we are depressed, confused, or angry, we can describe our thoughts and feelings without the passion that leads to unhealthy actions.

Traumatic Grief Therapy

This is a specialized type of grief therapy that deals specifically with traumatic grief—a type of grief that occurs after a very sudden or unexpected loss.

Traumatic grief was present in the example of Jane and Twinkie that we looked at in Chapter 3. Twinkie was just over a year old when she suddenly got sick. The vet was convinced it was nothing serious and that Twinkie would be fine after spending one night in the clinic. The next morning, Twinkie passed away. It was sudden and unexpected, and the pup still had her whole life ahead of her.

The suddenness causes trauma; a feeling of powerlessness in the face of circumstances. This causes physical and mental symptoms, including intrusive thoughts, trouble sleeping, loss of appetite, and anxiety.

Traumatic grief therapy focuses strongly on establishing a healthy routine to help regulate our emotions. We are encouraged to express ourselves freely (but in a healthy way) and to understand that what we're feeling is perfectly normal and to be expected.

In many cases, this type of grief must be dealt with as two separate occurrences—trauma and grief. Each must be treated on its own.

General Therapeutic Techniques

Regardless of the type of therapy required, therapists tend to use similar techniques to help us. Common techniques include:

- **Mindfulness-based therapy:** Mindfulness encourages people to stay present and aware of their thoughts and feelings without judgment. This helps manage overwhelming emotions and makes them easier to deal with and process.

- **Narrative therapy:** This technique focuses on people telling and re-telling the story of their pet's life and the bond they shared. This helps people find meaning in their pet's life and honor their memory.

- **Art therapy:** A technique that uses creative expression, such as drawing, painting, or writing to process emotions and express grief in non-verbal ways.

Does Counseling Really Work?

Many people wonder if counseling really works, either because they don't believe in the principles applied during therapy, or because they didn't see the results when they've been in therapy themselves.

The fact is that therapy and counseling help but there are several variables to consider. For example, some people don't necessarily connect with certain therapists in an effective way, which hinders the process. In some cases, the therapy was so subtle that the person might believe they "got over their problems" by themselves, not realizing that the therapist was instrumental in helping them understand what they had to do. In some ways, those are the best therapists. But having subtle results doesn't mean therapy doesn't work.

Science has proven over and over that grief counseling and therapy work. In fact, the results of five separate studies conducted over the span of two decades all found that approximately 79% of people who received grief counseling were better off after therapy than those who did not receive any type of counseling (Jordan & Neimeyer, n.d.).

In other words, it's important to ask for help if you need it. If grief goes untreated for too long, it can become unhealthy and could lead to other mental and emotional problems in the future.

Finding a Pet Loss Counselor

As we've seen, one of the reasons why many people feel that counseling and therapy don't work is that they don't have the right counselor. You need to find someone who understands the problem you're struggling with, and you should also feel comfortable with them.

Steps to Finding the Right Counselor

Any grief counselor will be able to help you with your current struggle, but a specialized pet loss counselor can provide more of the understanding and support you need during this difficult time. So, what should you do to find the right counselor?

Step 1: Determine Your Needs

Before beginning your search, take some time to consider what you are looking for in a counselor. Reflect on your specific needs and preferences by asking yourself questions like:

- Do you prefer individual counseling, group therapy, or a combination of both?

- Are you looking for a counselor with specific qualifications or experience in pet loss?

- Do you prefer in-person sessions, or are you open to virtual counseling?

- What is your budget for counseling services, or do you have insurance coverage that might help?

Step 2: Seek Recommendations

It's always a good idea to choose a therapist with a proven track record, and the best way to do that is by getting reliable recommendations. Start by asking for recommendations from friends and family, but you can also turn to trusted sources like:

- **Veterinarians:** Most veterinarians have experience with pet loss and can recommend counselors who specialize in this area.

- **Animal shelters:** Local animal shelters often have connections with pet loss counselors or can direct you to support groups.

Step 3: Research Online

The internet is a valuable resource with a nearly infinite list of pet loss counselors.

Websites like Psychology Today and the American Counseling Association have directories that allow you to search for counselors by specialization and location. Organizations such as the Association for Pet Loss and Bereavement (APLB) often have lists of recommended counselors and support groups. You will have no trouble finding a therapist online.

However, before you commit, read some reviews and testimonials to get insight into the experiences of other clients. This could help you find a counselor who is sure to be a good fit for you.

Step 4: Verify Credentials

It's sad to say, but even the world of grief counseling is full of charlatans and scammers looking for ways to make some "easy money." So, once you have identified potential counselors, it's important to verify their credentials before booking an appointment.

Look for the following:

- **Licensure:** Ensure that the counselor is licensed in your state. Licensed counselors have met specific educational and professional requirements according to local laws and regulations.

- **Specialization:** Check if the counselor has specific training or experience in grief counseling in general, and more specifically, pet loss.

- **Professional memberships:** Membership in professional organizations, such as the American Counseling Association or APLB, can indicate a commitment to ongoing education and maintaining ethical standards, which usually means they are more reliable and trustworthy.

This might seem a bit extreme, but your mental health and well-being is worth the extra effort.

Step 5: Get Important Information

There are some things you will have to confirm before committing to a counselor. Some allow preliminary consultations, while others have this information freely available on their websites, in brochures, or via a call to their receptionists. Ask questions such as:

- What experience do they have in dealing with pet loss? Is it a specialization field or, if not, have they ever helped someone with it?

- What counseling techniques do they use, and how might those techniques benefit you?

- What is their availability for sessions, and do they offer virtual or online options?

- What are their fees, and do they accept insurance?

Step 6: Trust Your Instincts

In the end, the type of relationship you form with your counselor is crucial. Therapy can be hard enough, so you don't want to have a therapist with a clashing personality type or who irritates you in some way. Trust your instincts when deciding if a counselor is right for you. You should feel comfortable, understood, and supported.

Resources for Finding a Pet Loss Counselor

Here are some resources that can help you in your search for a pet loss counselor.

- **Association for Pet Loss and Bereavement (APLB):** APLB offers a directory of pet loss counselors and support groups: https://www.aplb.org/

- **American Counseling Association (ACA):** ACA's directory allows you to search for licensed counselors by specialization and location: https://www.counseling.org/

- **Psychology Today:** This website has a comprehensive directory of therapists, including some who specialize in grief and pet loss: https://www.psychologytoday.com/intl/counsellors

- **BetterHelp:** This online platform and app has several verified and experienced counselors available for virtual sessions at the tap of a button. You can easily switch therapists if you feel you haven't found the right match. You can download the BetterHelp app on your smartphone, or visit betterhelp.com.

- **Pet Loss Support Hotlines**: Some veterinary schools and animal organizations offer pet loss support hotlines where you can get immediate support if you need it, as well as referrals to local counselors.

  - **Tufts University Pet Loss Support Hotline:** 508-839-7966

  - **Cornell University Pet Loss Support Hotline:** 607-218-7457

Tips for Choosing the Right Counselor

Finding the right counselor involves more than just verifying credentials and experience. Let's consider a few additional tips to ensure you choose the right one for you.

- **Comfort level:** It's essential to feel comfortable with your counselor. Your sessions should be a safe space where you can express your feelings openly while feeling heard and not judged in any way..

- **Communication style:** Ensure that the counselor's communication style matches your own preferences. Do they listen actively and respond with empathy? Do you understand one another clearly? Does the therapist ask you questions to elaborate on your feelings?

- **Therapeutic approach:** Different counselors use different therapeutic approaches, usually based on personal preference and experience. Make sure their methods align with your needs and requirements.

- **Cultural sensitivity:** Choose a counselor who respects and understands your cultural background and values.

- **Trial sessions:** Don't be afraid to try a few sessions with different counselors to find the best fit. It's important to find someone you can connect with on a personal level.

In Summary

We humans are very resilient creatures, but we aren't meant to face challenges alone. Reaching out for help doesn't make you weak. In fact, it takes a special kind of strength and tenacity to admit that you need a bit of support.

Friends and family are usually our first go-to options, but despite their best intentions, they don't always understand our situations enough to be really helpful. Support groups are a better option since you can open up to others who have gone through the same struggles and know exactly what you're talking about.

Grief counseling is also an excellent option, especially if you feel that the grief is becoming too much for you. It can easily lead to other mental health issues, so it's best to seek professional help when you need it.

But humans aren't the only ones affected by the loss of a pet—we often don't even realize how much it can affect our other pets. How can we help our other animals deal? That's what we'll be exploring in the next chapter.

Chapter 5:

Impact of Pet Loss on Other Pets

in the Home

You are intimately aware of the pain you're suffering after losing your pet. It's safe to assume that the pain is similar for your whole family because of how much your pet became a member of your household. We've seen that children may express their grief in different ways, but they also experience that pain and longing.

But some of our households are a bit more extended. Many of us have more than one pet and, since they are all members of the family, their bonds with each other can be just as strong. Yes, it's true that they may not get along all the time, but that's true of humans too, isn't it?

Dorothy is a widow I met several years ago. Her husband had passed away eight years before, and her kids were all married and had families of their own. Most of them lived far away and couldn't visit their mother very often. So, to combat her loneliness, Dorothy got a few pets–two dogs and a cat, to be exact.

The cat wasn't very sociable. She didn't like to be handled or played with much, so she mostly did her own thing. But the two dogs, Pete and Milly, were full-on lap dogs. They competed for Dorothy's attention and struggled to find the best spots to sit next to her on her couch. Pete was also very protective and would show his frustration whenever someone came close to Dorothy, but never in an aggressive way.

Dorothy adopted both dogs when they were puppies, within a week of each other, so they grew up together. They would play with each other often and generally got along well, but just like human siblings, they had their spats at times, especially when Dorothy would sit on the couch to watch TV, which was when they would for the spot closest to their mom.

After several years, when Dorothy was rapidly approaching the ripe old age of 80, Pete passed away. It happened suddenly; there was no warning, and the vet found it was a heart attack since Pete had a heart problem that was never detected during check-ups.

Dorothy was very upset and sad, which was understandable. Her pets had become like her children over the years. They kept her company and made her home feel less empty. But it took her a while to realize that Milly was suffering, too.

For the first few days, the only thing she noticed was that Milly kept looking for Pete. She walked around the house and sniffed in every corner, trying to find him. She destroyed Pete's bed, scratching it to shreds, trying to find him. Around the second day, she started crying. Small whines at first, but they turned into yelps of sadness. She stopped eating and would carry food to the spot where Pete used to laze in the sun. At night, when Dorothy sat down in front of the TV, Milly would be restless on her lap for a few minutes before eventually getting up and lying down next to Dorothy, whining softly.

Dorothy had never thought about it before, but that's when she realized pets also grieve the loss of their animal siblings, and it's something that should be dealt with in love.

But it's not exactly as if you can take your pet to a therapist, is it? There aren't dog support groups, after all. So, if your pets are struggling with grief, how can you help them deal with their heartache?

Understanding Pet Grief

Like the grief we experience as humans, pet grief is the emotional response that surviving pets experience after the loss of a companion.

The companion can be a fellow pet with whom they share a close bond, but it could also be a human family member.

While we often think of grief as a uniquely human experience, research and evidence have shown that many animals exhibit behaviors that indicate mourning and loss.

Pet grief manifests in various ways, depending on the species and personality of the pet as well as the circumstances surrounding the loss. Common symptoms and signs of grief in pets include:

- **Changes in behavior:** Surviving pets often become more withdrawn, aggressive, or clingy. They might search for the lost companion, vocalize more (through whines or yelps), or exhibit changes in their sleeping patterns. Signs of agitation are also common.

- **Loss of appetite:** A grieving pet will often refuse to eat or show a decreased interest in food.

- **Lethargy:** Pets may appear unusually tired or show a lack of interest in activities they once enjoyed.

- **Depression-like symptoms:** Similar to humans, pets can exhibit signs of depression like a lack of enthusiasm, reduced interaction with family members, or a generally subdued demeanor.

We will look at the signs in more detail in a moment, but it's important for us to realize that the grief our pets experience is every bit as real, valid, and intense as our own. In fact, scientific studies have found that various animal species show signs of grief, proving that it is not exclusively a human experience.

One notable study is captured in the book *How Animals Grieve* by Barbara J. King (2014), which explores numerous instances of animals displaying grief-like behaviors.

In her book, King discusses how elephants, known for their strong social bonds, have been seen to stand vigil over a deceased companion while exhibiting behaviors such as touching and caressing the body with their trunks. Similarly, many primates have been seen carrying the bodies of their deceased young for days or even weeks, which indicates a deep sense of loss and mourning.

Dogs, often considered man's best friend, are also known to grieve the loss of their human or animal companions. Even though cats are more independent by nature, they can also exhibit signs of grief. They may hide, lose interest in play, or become more vocal.

I'm sure you've heard the story of Hachi-Ko (often written as *Hachiko*), the Japanese Akita dog who became world-famous through a book written by Shizuko O. Koster (2007) and a subsequent movie starring Richard Gere.

Hachi was the dog of Professor Eizaburo Ueno, who commuted to and from work by train. Every day, Hachi would go to the train station to wait for Ueno to come home. When Ueno passed away unexpectedly at work in 1925, Hachi kept going back to the station to wait, every day, until he himself eventually passed away ten years later. His unwavering loyalty toward his owner caused the citizens of Japan to honor him with a statue at the station and refer to him as the Samurai dog.

Think about that for a moment. This dog remembered his owner and kept waiting for him, for a decade. With that kind of love and loyalty, can there be any doubt that pets can grieve?

Your pets' grief is just as real and intense as yours—and perhaps even more intense. Remember that they experience and exhibit the purest form of selfless and unconditional love, and their grief comes from that same character of innocence and purity.

Common Signs and Symptoms of Pet Grief

So, how can you know if your pet is grieving? Even though the signs may differ from pet to pet, there are a few common signs to look out for.

Understanding the common signs and symptoms of pet grief can help pet owners recognize when their surviving pets are struggling and need extra support. Here are some signs to watch for:

- **Changes in eating habits:** A grieving pet may lose interest in food or eat significantly less than usual. On the other hand, some pets might overeat as a coping mechanism.

- **Altered sleep patterns:** Your pets might sleep more than usual, which reflects a depressive state. Or they could have difficulty sleeping and display signs of restlessness and anxiety.

- **Increased vocalization:** Pets may become more vocal, cry out, or bark or meow more frequently, especially during times they previously shared with the deceased pet.

- **Social withdrawal:** A grieving pet may become more isolated, trying to avoid interactions with humans and other animals in the household.

- **Behavioral changes:** Pets often exhibit uncharacteristic behaviors. For example, they might become more aggressive or overly clingy as they struggle to understand the loss.

- **Searching for the lost pet:** It is not uncommon for pets to search for their missing companion. They will go looking in places where the deceased pet used to rest or play and get agitated or upset when they can't find them.

- **Loss of interest:** A grieving pet might lose interest in activities they once enjoyed, such as playing with toys or going for walks. Dogs that love to play fetch will often just ignore the ball or stick, and cats that enjoy playing with their scratching post might be completely uninterested in it.

- **Physical symptoms:** Some pets even develop physical symptoms like gastrointestinal issues or skin problems as a response to stress and grief. I've had a pet myself who developed diarrhea and began vomiting a few days after losing a companion.

In other words, our pets show signs of grief in many of the same ways we do. These changes can be upsetting to see. When we've just lost a pet, perhaps due to illness, we can quickly think the worst when our surviving pets show these signs. But don't jump to conclusions—keep in mind that pet grief is normal and very common. They need support to work through it, just like you, so keep an eye on them and try to help them through this time.

How to Help Your Pet Cope With Loss

Like us, our pets need some extra support to cope with their grief. In fact, while we are also grieving, our pets tend to suffer even more because not only are they sad and missing their companion, but they notice that there's something wrong with us, too.

The truth is, we as humans tend to underestimate the emotional depth that animals have. Yes, we understand that our pets love us. We realize that they experience the same emotions we do—love, anger, fear, and sadness. But we underestimate how deeply those emotions affect them. In his book *The Emotional Lives of Animals* (2008), Marc Bekoff shares proof that animals have the same emotional range as humans and can experience all the things we do (including grief) in exactly the same way. We should not consider our pets' grief any less than our own. This means they also need all the support and care they can get, and it is up to us to provide them with that.

The good news is, there's a lot we can do to help our furry family members cope. They need a nurturing environment, and we can help create that for them.

Spend More Time With Them

One of the most important ways to support a grieving pet is by spending more quality time with them. The increased companionship and attention can offer comfort and reassurance during this challenging period. Interestingly, that works both ways. As we spend more time with our pets to comfort them, they also comfort us.

Engage in activities your pet enjoys, such as playing, walking, or simply sitting together. Physical touch, like petting and cuddling, can be particularly soothing. But it's also important to encourage positive interaction by being patient and gentle. Avoid forcing your pet into activities they are not interested in since this can add to their stress.

Maintain a Routine

Remember how we said one of the most important tips in dealing with your own grief is maintaining some form of routine? Routines help us understand that life goes on despite how we feel. It gives us a sense of structure and security during times of emotional turmoil. When everything else is shaken and seems uncertain, a routine helps us feel stable.

A routine is just as crucial for our pets since they thrive on predictability. For example, if they're used to being fed at a certain time every day, they will start asking for food when that time draws near. A stable routine can provide a sense of security and normalcy while they're working through emotions they don't understand.

Keep your normal feeding, walking, and playtime schedules as consistent as possible. This helps create a structured environment that can help to ease their anxiety. Also, try to keep their home environment unchanged. Avoid making significant changes, such as rearranging furniture or introducing new pets too soon. Too many drastic changes could further unsettle your grieving pet.

Offer Distractions

You can help distract your pet from their grief and provide mental stimulation by introducing new toys or engaging in new activities with them. This is essential for their emotional well-being.

Try to find interactive toys to fascinate them. Puzzle toys and treat-dispensing toys can keep your pet entertained and mentally engaged to provide a healthy distraction from their grief.

Consider participating in new activities that your pet might enjoy, such as agility training for dogs or new climbing structures for cats. These activities will help redirect their focus and energy.

A former colleague of mine had two dogs. Since he had a big yard, he never felt the need to take them out for walks—they would simply walk and run around in the yard. When one of his dogs passed away, he and his surviving dog went through their grief together.

One day he felt the urge to take his dog out for a walk, so that's what he did. The dog thought it was his birthday. He loved every minute of it, experiencing all the new sights and smells that he had never had access to. Seeing his dog's joy helped lift my colleague's spirits as well. The change of scenery was a therapeutic experience for both of them, and it soon became a regular part of their routine.

Offer Comforting Items

Remember that our pets rely very strongly on their sense of smell, so it's a good idea to give them items that contain the smell of their lost companion. Consider giving them old toys, blankets, pillows, jerseys, or anything else that the lost pet used. You might find that they often spend time with those items to find comfort.

It's also a good idea to allow them to lie down in areas where their lost companion spent a lot of time. Again, the scent will comfort them and help them work through their grief.

I mentioned Dorothy and Milly at the beginning of this chapter. After Pete passed away, Milly wasn't really interested in playing at all. She ignored her toys and all of Dorothy's attempts to distract her. Eventually, Dorothy gave up trying and simply decided to give Milly comfort. When they were in front of the TV at night, she would wrap Pete's old blanket around Milly and gently stroke her fur. This would eventually calm Milly down and help her sleep for a while.

Sometimes, we can find the greatest peace in simple things. Have you ever felt the comfort of a hug after a long and hard day? Or the joy of finally getting into bed after struggling with something for hours? Sometimes that's all our pets need, too. Never underestimate the power of simple comforts.

When Simple Measures Are Not Enough

As humans, many of us manage to work through the grief on our own when given enough time. Especially being aware of the signs and what to expect can help drive us in the right direction. The same is true of our pets—when we are considerate of their grief and provide the necessary comfort, they tend to work through it. But, as with us, there are times when professional help might be necessary. So how do you know if your pet needs some assistance? And who can you turn to to make that happen?

Let's go into that in more detail.

When to Seek Professional Help

Just a few decades ago, people would have considered you a bit crazy if you went looking for a professional to help your pet cope with grief. Some people might still think that way, but as the world discovers more evidence about our pets' emotional needs, we are opening up to new possibilities. These days we have access to professionals who can help our pets when they are struggling, or when we don't know what to do anymore.

Identifying the Need for Professional Help

It's important to monitor your pet closely and recognize when their grief may be overwhelming their ability to function normally. Here are some signs to indicate that it might be necessary to seek professional help.

Refusal to Eat or Drink

Loss of appetite is normal during grief, so don't immediately think the worst. But if your pet refuses to eat or drink for an extended period, it could lead to serious health complications. A prolonged lack of appetite can result in significant weight loss, dehydration, and malnutrition. So, there are two things to look out for:

- **Extended duration:** If your pet hasn't eaten or drunk anything for more than 24 to 48 hours, it's time to seek veterinary advice (Godfrey, 2022). This is especially true if they don't drink any water at all. Pets can go without food for a bit longer, but like humans, drinking water is absolutely vital.

- **Inadequate intake:** Even if they are eating or drinking a little, but not enough to maintain their health, this warrants professional attention. Contact a vet to get advice on medication that can help stimulate their appetite.

Extreme Behavioral Changes

Their behavior will change; it is a normal part of the grieving process. However, significant or drastic changes in behavior can be a clear indication that your pet is struggling too much with their grief. Behavioral changes might include:

- **Aggression:** Increased aggression towards other pets or family members is never a good sign, so it indicates that action should be taken.

- **Destructiveness:** Engaging in destructive behaviors like chewing furniture, scratching excessively, or damaging household items. These behaviors are often associated with separation anxiety, which is one aspect of pet grief.

- **Excessive vocalization:** Unusual or increased vocalization, such as howling, barking, or meowing, especially at night. Again, keep in mind that they will probably be more vocal than usual, but if it becomes excessive, it's time to seek professional help.

- **Separation anxiety:** Your pet will probably show increased clinginess or distress when left alone because they are used to having their companion with them when you're not there. However, most pets should get used to it fairly quickly, so if the separation anxiety becomes extreme or carries on for too long, it's a good idea to call a professional.

Prolonged Lethargy or Disinterest

If your pet remains unusually lethargic or disinterested in their surroundings for an extended period, it usually indicates a deeper level of emotional distress which should be treated by a professional. Look out for the following:

- **Lack of energy:** This shows itself in persistent lethargy, where the pet shows no interest in play, walks, or any activities they previously enjoyed, especially if it continues for several days. As they work through grief in a healthy way, they should become more energetic. If it doesn't happen, it's a sign that there are problems.

- **Withdrawal:** If they continuously withdraw from social interactions with family members or other pets, call a professional. For example, if they were usually excited to see a particular visitor and suddenly show no interest, they are withdrawing too much.

Resources for Finding Professional Help

As mentioned, it's important to keep the balance. Those signs are all normal up to a point, but if they get extreme, there are many places you can turn to for help.

Veterinarians

Your first point of contact should always be your veterinarian. They probably know your pet's background, so they will recognize that something's wrong. They can provide a thorough health check to rule out any physical health issues that might be exacerbating your pet's grief. Veterinarians can also offer advice on managing grief and may prescribe medication or supplements if needed.

Schedule an appointment to do a comprehensive health check. While you're there, discuss your pet's behavior and get a few recommendations for managing their grief.

Animal Behaviorists

In modern times, we have certified animal behaviorists that are professionally trained and specialize in understanding and addressing behavioral issues in pets, including the signs of excessive grief. They can help you by providing personalized strategies and training to help your pet cope.

As you would when looking for a therapist for yourself, it's important to find the right person. Look for certified applied animal behaviorists (CAAB) or veterinary behaviorists (DACVB). The certification proves that they are qualified to help your pet. When you make an appointment, discuss the situation and ensure that they are experienced in the specific problems your pet is facing. This way, you can engage in behavioral therapy sessions tailored to your pet's needs.

Pet Loss Counselors

Many pet loss counselors specialize in helping not just pet owners, but also their pets, navigate the grieving process. Because they are experienced in dealing with the intricacies of pet loss, they can offer emotional support and practical advice on helping your pet cope with the loss of their companion.

When you look for pet loss counselors, try to find counseling services that offer support for both pet owners and pets. You can also participate in support groups that are facilitated by pet loss counselors to share experiences and gain insights because it's likely that some of the other attendees have faced (and overcome) the same challenges you're facing.

Pet Loss Support Hotlines

Many organizations offer hotlines where you can speak to professionals about your pet's grief and get advice or referrals for more hands-on help. These hotlines provide immediate support and can guide you in finding the best resources.

You can reach out to any of the hotlines we mentioned in Chapter 4 to get immediate emotional support and valuable guidance. You can also ask for referrals from friends, family, or your vet to find local professionals or support groups that can help.

How Effective Are These Methods?

We always want the best for our pets, don't we? They are family members, friends, and some of our closest companions. With that in mind, it's easy to wonder if these methods and treatments are really effective, so let's look at some real-life examples.

Charlie is a Labrador Retriever. He and his brother, Pepper, were both adopted by Greg and his wife, Amanda, when they were six weeks old. The two grew up together and were best friends. Greg and Amanda never had any kids, so Charlie and Pepper were the children in their home.

When they were about six years old, Pepper became quite sick. He had always been a little bit sickly, so his parents didn't think too much of it at first, but when his problems continued for two days, they took him to the vet. Sadly, Pepper died in the car on the way. They still took him to the vet and, in tears, made the necessary arrangements to have him cremated.

Charlie saw them put Pepper in the car and leave, so when they returned and opened the car door, Charlie jumped in and started looking for Pepper. When he couldn't find him he jumped out again and started running around the car, looking for his companion. This carried on for several minutes until Greg and Amanda finally managed to get him back into the house.

The poor dog spent the rest of the day sniffing around and whining because he couldn't find his brother. Greg and Amanda did everything they could to calm him down, but nothing helped.

Over the next two days, they noticed that Charlie refused to eat. Whenever they put down his bowl, he would get up to check if Pepper was there. Not seeing his brother, he would turn around and slump down into his bed without taking a single bite. Even though they realized it was normal and weren't immediately concerned about his health, they decided it was a good idea to talk to the vet.

Recognizing the signs of grief, the vet immediately prescribed some anti-anxiety medication. It was quite a struggle, but Greg and Amanda eventually managed to get Charlie to take his medicine. That night Charlie had the best sleep he'd had in a few days, and the next morning he started eating. His appetite returned and his energy levels improved, and he gradually became his old self again.

Cleo was a senior cat who had been living with Judy and Rob for more than 12 years. She was a quiet and loving cat. She didn't enjoy petting very much, but she would always curl up on the lap of any person she could find. Judy and Rob had two other cats and a dog as well, but they all got along well and Cleo never had problems with any of her companions.

When one of the other cats, Tilly, died, Cleo didn't really show signs of grief. She ate more or less as she always had, and her lifestyle didn't change much in any way. However, a few days after Tilly's passing, Judy heard hissing and yelping from the living room. She ran in to see what was going on and found that Cleo had attacked their young dog, Buddy. The pup sat trembling in the corner, as far away from Cleo as possible, with a bloody welt across his nose where the cat attacked him.

Judy didn't think too much of it at the time. It was strange for Cleo, but pets often have fights and disagreements, and it would blow over eventually, so she cleaned Buddy's wound and checked that everything was okay.

That night, while they were watching TV, Buddy walked up to Rob's side of the couch and got ready to jump up. Suddenly, a Cleo-shaped comet zoomed hissing over the couch and hit poor Buddy in the face again. That's when Judy and Rob realized something was wrong.

The next morning, Judy called the vet and told him about the problems. The vet told her that it was probably Cleo's way of expressing her grief. He prescribed mild anti-anxiety medication and gave Judy the number of an animal behaviorist nearby.

The behaviorist came over and observed Cleo, especially the way she interacted with the other pets, and confirmed that her aggression was caused by grief. He guided Judy and Rob on ways to help Cleo change the behavior, which involved separating the pets at certain times and doing specific activities. He also told them not to try and console Cleo when she became aggressive because cats tend to perceive that as approval of the aggression. Instead, they were to ignore Cleo at those times and focus their attention on the other pets.

Over time, this helped. Cleo used the medication for about two weeks, after which the behavioral therapy had worked its magic, and the pets all got along again.

In other words, therapy can definitely help your pets cope with the effects of grief. Not all pets need it, but if they do, a combination of medication and behavioral therapy can do wonders for their emotional turmoil. Our pets may not look like us, but emotionally, we really aren't that different.

The Importance of Timely Intervention

Have you ever had one of those experiences where you were hesitant to take action, possibly not believing it was really necessary, but now you wish you had done something sooner? Perhaps you're feeling that way about the death of your pet, believing you could have taken action when you saw the first signs of trouble (remember, that's the bargaining stage of grief in action).

The fact is, sometimes it's best to take action when we see the first signs. If your pet is struggling with grief, there's a good chance that everything will work out fine on their own. Things usually work out like that, so it's normal to believe there's no reason to be concerned.

But let's consider the other possibility for a moment. If your pets are having trouble eating, how long can that carry on before they develop serious health issues? If they've become aggressive in an attempt to vent their frustrations, what could go wrong if you don't intervene?

It's absolutely crucial to take steps as soon as possible. When you notice signs of trouble, call your vet. Reach out to animal grief services. Get professional opinions. Most likely, everything is okay, which means you can relax. But if things aren't okay, you know that you're doing everything in your power to help improve your pet's mental health.

Considering the pros and cons, wouldn't you rather get professional assistance and not really need it, than not getting it and realizing later that it was actually important?

In Summary

Animals have a wide emotional spectrum. They experience joy, sadness, anger, humiliation, and grief just like we do. When you lose a pet, they also lose a family member, friend, and companion. They will grieve every bit as much as you do.

We can easily feel overwhelmed by the power and intensity of our grief, but we can use logic to reason things out to some extent. Our pets, on the other hand, don't understand why their companion is no longer there. Their behavior and habits will change as they try to make sense of this new empty life.

It's up to us to take care of our pets' emotional well-being. We can guide them through their grief by keeping routines, offering distractions, and providing lots of comfort and love. And, if things get too difficult, professionals like vets and animal behaviorists can step in to help us find the best ways to help our beloved pets.

Chapter 6:

Deciding When to Adopt a New

Pet

Losing a pet causes a rush of thoughts and emotions that we could never have expected or prepared for. Not only do we have immense sadness, depression, and the painful realization that we will never see our pets again, but everywhere we look, we are reminded of their presence and the void they left behind. We feel empty, hopeless, and so, so lonely.

To make matters worse, there are also the more physical aspects of their loss. The empty spot on the couch next to you, the absence of pattering paws on the kitchen floor, and the silence in your home as you make your way to bed at night, all reflect the void in your heart.

It's common for people who just lost a pet to have two vastly opposing thoughts. Most of us go through a phase where we vow to never get another pet, because we simply can't go through this pain again. But not long after that, and often at the same time, we realize that getting a new pet will help fill at least some of the void in our hearts and homes. Yes, it's true that no other pet could ever replace the one we've lost. They had their own character and personality which brought life into the home. But a new pet will take away that silence, help bring us comfort, and bring the house to life with *their* unique personality.

But is it a good idea? Aren't you just projecting your pain onto a new creature that deserves more than that? If it is a good idea, when is the best time to do so, and what aspects should you consider as you take that step?

Let's explore the process of adopting a new pet while suffering through your grief.

When Is It Too Soon?

One of the questions people most often wonder is, is it too soon to get a new pet? Unfortunately, I have to tell you that there is no definite, clear answer. It is largely up to you. But that doesn't make the question any less important. Adopting a pet is a big decision that impacts you and your family in crucial ways, but even more than that, there's a pet to consider. A living being with its own feelings, thoughts, and emotions, potentially caught in the middle of a grieving family. That doesn't necessarily make it a bad thing; it could be good for you and your family and cause no negative feelings toward the pet. But it's crucial to consider all sides of the story before perhaps making a mistake.

Consider the Grieving Process

We've gone through the grieving process in considerable detail in earlier chapters, but when deciding if it's time to get a new pet, keep the process in mind. Which of the five stages are you going through? Where are you in your healing process? What about your family members and other pets? We don't all go through grief at the same pace, so it's important to consider everyone in your decision.

We can't specify with any certainty how long grief lasts because it is such a personal matter. People usually start to feel better after about six months, but it usually takes up to two years to fully heal after losing a loved one (Cox, 2016). That time is full of emotional ups and downs. You could go through days or weeks at a time without feeling any grief or sadness, then a sudden memory will pop up and trigger a new wave of depression.

The fact that you feel you've moved on doesn't mean everyone in your household has. Talk to them. Make this a family conversation.

Consider your other pets and how they might experience the introduction of a new pet into the home. They might also be going through grief and become aggressive toward a newcomer.

Jim and Angela are a happily married couple with one son. Jim grew up in a household with plenty of dogs, and after getting married, they always had at least one dog in their home. As a result, their son also grew up with dogs around him, so he considered them members of the family.

Over a two-year period, all their dogs passed away, leaving just one young puppy they had recently adopted. The small family invested all their love and attention in this one doggy, to the extent that some people considered her spoiled, though that wasn't really the case. They simply had a lot of love to give, and only one dog to give it to. During this time, they never even considered getting another pet.

Unfortunately, when she was two years old, the puppy had an accident and died. Obviously the family was devastated. The grief was almost unbearable and the worst they had ever experienced, but Jim and Angela both found the silence in their home to be one of the hardest parts to cope with. They both worked from home, and everything was just too quiet and lonely without their constant companion.

About two months after the passing of their pup, they decided it was time to adopt a new dog. They felt it was the right time. They discussed that the new pet wouldn't be a replacement, since that was impossible—she would be a new pet in her own right, but she would help fill part of the void and break the silence a bit.

Unfortunately, they made a big mistake by not discussing it with their son first. He's a quiet twelve-year-old who doesn't really talk about his feelings much, and they mistakenly believed he would be okay with having a new dog. As it turned out, he wasn't.

When they brought the new puppy home to surprise him, he took one look at her and, with tears streaming down his face, locked himself in his bedroom. No amount of pleading from his parents got him out of his room for the rest of the day. Over the next few days he would come out for meals and to go to school, but apart from that, he kept to himself. When he was with his family during meals, he ignored the dog completely and didn't even acknowledge her existence. Jim tried to talk to him, but he just said "I don't want to talk about it."

After several weeks with no change or improvement, Jim decided it was time to take his son to a therapist because it was obvious he was struggling. It didn't take long to get to the bottom of the problem: their son felt like they were trying to replace the puppy he had loved so much, and he couldn't betray her like that.

Over time, and with the help of the therapist and his loving parents, he discovered that that wasn't the case. This was simply a new family member, not a replacement in any way. Loving a new dog didn't mean rejecting the memory of the one who passed away; love is not a limited commodity, and he had enough love in his heart to care for both pets. He eventually welcomed the new puppy into their home and accepted her as a family member.

The story has a happy ending, but Jim and Angela could have saved the whole family a lot of pain by just talking to their son first and explaining their reasons for adopting a new pet. If they had considered his grief and helped him work through it first, they would have been able to receive the new pet into a home that was ready to receive her.

Perhaps the most common concern is feeling guilty or disloyal to the pet you lost. You might worry that bringing a new pet into your home too soon would dishonor the memory of your lost companion, which stems from the deep bond and the profound love you had for your pet. This is normal and healthy, but it's important to remember that grieving and opening your heart to a new pet are not mutually exclusive. Loving another pet does not diminish the love you had for the one you've lost.

For example, if you have multiple pets, do you love any of the others less when one of them passes? Does your love for the one who died diminish your affection for any of the others? Of course not. So, why would adopting a new pet be any different?

Some people find that adopting a new pet soon after their loss helps them cope with their grief. The presence of a new pet can provide comfort, a sense of routine, and a new focus for their attention and affection. For many, having a new pet to care for can ease the pain and help fill the void left by their loss. Cuddling up in front of the TV with a new pet can help soothe the pain you feel.

On the other hand, some people who adopt a new pet too soon may feel overwhelmed or find it challenging to bond with the new pet, as they are still deeply mourning their loss. It's best to ensure that the decision to adopt again is made with a clear mind and a healed heart, rather than as an attempt to quickly fill the emotional void.

So, the point is not to avoid adopting a new pet while you're grieving. Simply be aware of the grieving process of everyone in your household, humans and pets, and make decisions based on that. Consider the options clearly, discuss them with your family, and don't make any rash, emotional decisions.

Indicators That It Might Be Too Soon

Adopting a new pet should feel like a positive and joyful decision, not one made out of a sense of obligation or desperation. Let's consider some signs that it might be too soon to bring a new pet into your home.

- **Emotional overwhelm:** If the thought of adopting a new pet brings more anxiety than excitement, it might be a sign that you need more time to heal. Grieving is a process that cannot be rushed, and it's crucial to allow yourself the time you need to fully experience and process your emotions.

- **Constant comparisons:** When you start exploring the options, pay attention to how you do it. If you find yourself constantly comparing potential new pets to your deceased ones, it could be an indication that you are not ready. Each pet is unique, and it's important to welcome a new companion for who they are, not as a replacement for your lost pet. Embrace their unique traits and characteristics rather than trying to duplicate those of the pet you lost.

- **Unresolved grief:** If your grief still feels raw and overwhelming, it might be best to wait. The process of mourning and healing varies for everyone, and it's essential to honor your feelings and take the time you need. This is also important for your new pet. Remember that our pets detect our emotions, and experiencing the raw sadness and depression we are going through is not the best way for a new pet to feel welcome and loved.

When you're pondering if it's too soon to adopt a new pet, balance your emotional readiness with practical considerations. Ensure you are ready to provide the necessary care, attention, and love a new pet deserves. Take the time to reflect on your emotions and ask for support from your friends, family members, or pet loss support groups if needed. However, as you do so, keep in mind that we all handle it differently, and whatever you decide to do, commit to it fully. If you decide it's time to get a new pet, know that it's a commitment for life, regardless of whether you are ready or not.

The Right Time

After saying all of that, remember that it's not a matter of *never* getting a new pet; it's all about choosing the right time. Your grief is one determining factor in that, but there are also several other ways to know if the time is right for you to adopt a new furball. Let's go through those factors in more detail.

Signs You Might Be Ready for Another Pet

When you notice these signs in your life, it could indicate that you're ready for a new pet.

- **Missing animal companionship:** One of the most telling signs that you might be ready for a new pet is the longing for that specific type of companionship you can only get from a pet. When you find yourself missing the presence, routine, and joy that a pet brings, it may be an indication that your heart is opening up to the idea of another animal companion. Just check that you are truly missing the presence of *any* pet, and not specifically that of the pet you've lost.

- **Feeling lonely without a pet:** We all know how pets tend to become integral members of our families, and we are painfully aware of the fact that their absence can leave a significant void. If your home feels unusually quiet, or you feel a deep sense of loneliness, these feelings might suggest that you are ready to bring another pet into your life. Be careful to differentiate between those feelings and the feeling of loss you're experiencing, though. They are not mutually exclusive, so it's easy to confuse them at times.

- **Emotional stability:** Grief is a complex process that involves experiencing a range of emotions, and you can quickly switch from one emotion to another as you work through it. Introducing a new pet to that emotional rollercoaster is generally not a good idea. When you start to feel more emotionally stable and can think about your lost pet with fondness rather than overwhelming sadness, it might be a sign that you are ready to adopt again. Being emotionally ready means you can fully invest in a new pet and provide the love and care they need and deserve.

- **Readiness for responsibility:** We've seen that grief can interfere with our responsibilities and routines, and adopting a new pet comes with several new commitments. If you feel prepared to take on these responsibilities again and are excited about the prospect of caring for a new pet, it could be a sign that you are ready to adopt.

Steve was a successful, career-driven young man. Because of the demands of his job and his desire to climb the corporate ladder, he never really invested much time into dating and his social life. He had a few friends that he met up with on occasion, but for the most part, his cat, Smokey, was his closest companion.

He was given the opportunity for a significant promotion, but it meant he had to relocate to a city in a different state. With his priorities being what they were, he didn't even hesitate—he left his friend group behind and moved across the country to start a new life, taking only his cat with him. The new city was a bit intimidating and, since he never felt the need for social interactions outside of work, he never really went out, choosing to invest his care and attention into his cat. It wasn't necessarily the best choice, but it was his choice to make, and he was happy with it for a while.

Unfortunately, Smokey passed away about six months after he moved. Steve was devastated, but he had about two weeks' worth of annual leave saved up, which he used to get some time off to mourn his beloved companion.

It wasn't an easy process. During those two weeks, Steve kept to himself, never really leaving his home, and fell out of his routine. He went several days without taking a shower and would only eat when he realized that he had to because he had no appetite. He had no friends nearby to check in on him, so he was left to his own devices. To make matters worse, everywhere he turned he was reminded of Smokey in some way.

About a week after losing Smokey, he realized that he could fill the void by getting a new cat. He started browsing the Facebook page of an animal shelter nearby and looked at the photos of kittens that were up for adoption. He fell in love with several of them but was frustrated that none of the kittens were a perfect fit. After some self-reflection, he realized what the problem was. He wasn't looking for a cat; he was looking for Smokey. That realization drove home the fact that nothing he did could bring Smokey back. No other kitten would be Smokey, and expecting that of them was unfair to himself and his new pet.

Steve made what was probably one of the best decisions he could have made at the time: he closed Facebook and called up one of his new colleagues who he got along quite well with, inviting him to go out for a drink that night. The two chatted for several hours over drinks, and Steve actually felt good when he got home and had his first good night's sleep in more than a week.

Over the next few months, Steve and his colleague became good friends, and he even made friends with several other people in the area. He started going out more often and got involved in the community.

About eight months after Smokey died, Steve got home after a night with friends and realized that his home was too quiet. He didn't enjoy going home alone, and for the first time in months, he thought about adopting a new cat. He opened Facebook and found the page of the local animal shelter. This time he noticed a kitten that he immediately fell in love with, and three days later, he took his new pet home. She wasn't Smokey, but that was fine—Steve didn't expect her to be.

Embracing the Right Time

So, deciding on the right time to adopt a new pet involves listening to your emotions, filtering them through a logical reasoning process, and recognizing when you are ready. Take your time; there's no rush, and it's important to honor your grieving process. Let's look at a few tips to help you determine if now is the right time for you.

- **Self-reflection:** Spend time reflecting on your feelings and thoughts. When you think about adopting a new pet, how does it make you feel? What are the thoughts and emotions that trigger that desire? Journaling can be a helpful tool to explore your emotions and assess your readiness, so make notes of everything you think and feel.

- **Support system:** Talk to your friends, family, or support groups about your thoughts on adopting again. Their insights and encouragement can provide valuable perspective, and you may even find that social interaction helps fill the void that you want to fill with a new pet, just like Steve did.

- **Take your time:** Don't feel pressured to adopt too quickly. You might see a photo of a pet you love, and that's okay; if you want to adopt, go ahead. But remember that there will always be new pets looking for homes, so don't feel rushed. Allow yourself the time you need to heal and ensure that your decision is made with a clear mind and open heart.

- **Celebrate memories:** Adopting a new pet does *not* mean replacing the one you lost. So, as you're preparing yourself and your home for a new pet, create a special way to honor your lost pet's memory. Memorialize them in some loving, meaningful way. This will help you find peace and, over time, you will feel more ready to welcome a new pet into your life.

Factors to Consider Before Getting Another Pet

When you begin to suspect that you are ready for another pet, there are a few other matters to consider as well, because adopting a new pet is a significant decision that requires careful planning. While the desire to fill the void left by your lost pet is probably strong, it's important to think about various factors to ensure that both you and the new pet are happy and well-suited to each other.

- **Emotional readiness:** Before adopting another pet, check if you and your family (including other pets) are ready. As we already mentioned, it's important to consider whether you have processed your grief and are prepared to form a new bond without constantly comparing the new pet to the one you lost.

- **Practical considerations:** Think about the practical aspects of pet ownership. Consider your current lifestyle, work schedule, and financial situation to ensure you can provide the necessary care and attention to a new pet. Many things can change in the months you spend working through your grief, so it's important not to assume you are ready because you could have done it before.

- **Space and environment:** Assess your living space to determine if it's suitable for a new pet. Different pets have different needs, so ensure your home environment can still accommodate those needs.

- **Household dynamics:** Consider the dynamics of your household, including other pets and family members. Is everyone on board with the decision to adopt and ready to welcome a new pet? It's also helpful to think back on the last time you adopted a pet. What difficulties did you face? Could the same challenges happen again?

- **Financial responsibility:** Ensure you are financially prepared for the long-term costs associated with pet ownership, including food, medical care, grooming, and other supplies. Of course, nobody knows what will happen in the future, but it's important to know that you are doing everything you can to provide for your pet.

- **Time and attention:** Reflect on your ability to provide the time and attention your new pet will need. Pets thrive on interaction and companionship, so it's crucial for you to be prepared to invest this into your pet.

The decision-making process deserves careful attention. After all, you want to give your new pet the best home possible, so it's worth investing time and effort. A study by K. Haude et. al. (2016) describes a detailed process for decision-making in cases with long-term impacts. Though pet adoption wasn't the study's focus, the same principles apply. It involves considering the following three aspects that you can use to help you decide if you're ready for a new pet:

Step 1: Examine Your Expectations and Motivations

Why do you want to adopt a pet? What is driving you to the decision? Is it an emotional response, or are you still in favor of the decision when you think rationally and eliminate emotions from the equation?

What do you expect to get out of adopting a new pet? Do you expect the new pet to be the same (or similar) to the one you lost? Or do you simply expect them to become a new family member and companion?

Ask yourself these questions, then weigh your responses against the points we've discussed to see if your expectations are realistic and your motivations are healthy.

Step 2: Examine Support Systems

This aspect is crucial for you and your pet.

First, do you have the resources (such as time, space, and money) to care for the pet? Are there ways to care for the pet when you're unable to do so yourself?

Are you in a position where you can care for your pet emotionally as a unique individual, or are you still too caught up in grief?

These questions will help you determine if you're ready for a new pet on a more practical level.

Step 3: Consider the Long-Term Effects

When you adopt a pet, you're making a lifetime commitment. Yes, their lifetime isn't as long as yours, but you're committing to be there for them throughout their life. Are you ready for that? Do you have future plans that could ruin it?

I met a 70-year-old retired gentleman several years ago. He was a widower and all of his kids were either married or in college. His youngest son, Paul, was in his final year of college and technically still living at home when he adopted a dog without talking to his dad about it. Paul promised that he would take care of the pup and would not dump her on his father.

Two years later, Paul and his girlfriend decided to move in together and rented a small apartment that wasn't pet-friendly. Guess what? Paul left his dog in his father's care.

Thankfully his dad had gotten to love the dog by then. They were inseparable. But that doesn't change the fact that Paul should have considered the implications that his actions would have. The dog formed a bond with Paul, which Paul just shrugged off to someone else. It was not fair to the pup.

Remember, you have a life outside of your home and family, but your pet doesn't. You are all they have, and pets don't find it easy when they feel like the people they have a bond with, rejected them.

If you are planning a significant life change in the next few years (or longer), think about how that will affect your pet, and keep them in mind as you plan the next steps of your life.

How to Choose Your Next Pet

If you've gone through all the introspection and determined that you are ready to adopt a new pet, where do you start? Maybe it's been years since you adopted your last pet and you feel a bit lost. Let's explore the process in more detail.

Factors to Consider

- **Type of pet:** This is an important point to consider. It's likely you're thinking of adopting the same type of pet you've lost, but that doesn't necessarily have to be the case. Think about other options and weigh up the pros and cons before making a final decision.

- **Breed:** Research the different breeds to find one that matches your lifestyle and preferences. Consider factors like energy levels, grooming needs, size, and temperament.

- **Age:** Decide whether you want a puppy or kitten, an adult pet, or a senior pet. Each age group has its own benefits and unique challenges.

- **Temperament:** Consider the temperament of the new pet and how it will fit with your personality and the dynamics of your household.

- **Adoption options:** Explore various adoption options, such as rescue organizations, animal shelters, and reputable breeders. We'll look at that more closely in a moment.

Adoption Options

Once you've decided on the type of pet you want, it's time to start looking for the right pet. Here are a few popular options.

- **Friends, family, or breeders:** Sometimes getting a pet is as easy as reaching out to friends and family. Some of them might know of a reputable breeder or someone whose pets recently had babies. This isn't always the most reliable option since it can be a bit unpredictable, but it is an easy (and, often, very affordable) way to adopt a new pet.

- **Petfinder.com:** Petfinder is a popular website that lists pets that are up for adoption from a wide range of different shelters and organizations. You can easily search for the type and breed you're looking for and filter the results according to city and state. All listings on Petfinder are urgent; these animals are actively looking for new homes.

- **ASPCA:** The American Society for the Prevention of Cruelty to Animals provides many resources and adoption opportunities. You can usually visit your local ASPCA and get to meet numerous pets that are up for adoption.

- **Local shelters:** There are animal shelters all over the world. These shelters take care of animals that are abandoned or brought to the shelter by people who can't take care of them anymore. You can find different types and breeds, as well as various age groups, so it's usually pretty easy to find the perfect pet you're looking for by visiting a local shelter.

In Summary

Deciding to adopt a new pet after losing one is a difficult choice. Maybe you're not ready to even consider that possibility yet; that's fine. It's important to keep your current emotional state in mind while considering the needs of your family. The choice is up to you and your household, and what works for one person won't necessarily work for another.

If you want to adopt, think about your grieving process and the reasons why you want to adopt a new pet. Also, consider your current situation and where you plan to go in your life. When you decide to adopt, it's a life-long commitment, and it's crucial for you to be ready for that when the time comes. Don't feel pressured into making a decision; make it when you're ready.

Conclusion

As we reach the end of this book, I understand that it might have seemed like it was full of doom and gloom. After all, the topic of pet loss is not an easy one to discuss. You are suffering through immense pain right now, and it probably seems like nobody understands why it's so difficult for you—after all, it was "just a pet."

But I trust that, even though you probably cried often as you read these pages, the message I conveyed to you was one of hope. There is light at the end of the tunnel. The pain you're going through right now is normal, and it will pass eventually.

We saw that our pets are more than just animals. They are family members in every sense of the word. Their unconditional love and acceptance, along with the fact that they are so actively present in our lives, mean that they are every bit as important to us as any other person in our households. When we lose such a dear loved one, it's only normal to suffer immense pain and grieve over them as we would for anyone else.

So the grieving process is unpredictable. We don't know how long it will take, because it's different for each person. But we know that there are five stages, which gives us hope because we can see how far along we are in the grieving process. We can see that the emotions and thoughts we experience are normal and that we are not alone in our struggles.

We also saw that there are several things we can do to help us grieve. Memorializing our pets is a crucial step that shouldn't be underestimated because it gives us a sense of comfort and a way to honor the ones that brought us so much joy.

As normal as grief is, we also spoke about the fact that it can become unhealthy at times. Prolonged or extended grief can cause problems for our mental and emotional well-being. In those cases, we can get help from support groups or therapists. As strange as it might seem to some, there are professionals who specialize in helping people cope with the grief of losing a beloved pet. They are there to help us, and it's important for us to know when we should seek out that support.

But we should also consider the emotional well-being of the others in our homes. Our families, children, and even other pets will all go through grief in their own ways. For our human family members, we have the same options that we have ourselves—therapists and support groups. We can also support one another as we go through this difficult time. But we saw that our surviving pets may also need professional help to cope with the loss of an animal companion, and we can reach out to vets or animal behaviorists for that.

In other words, we know that this is a difficult time, full of darkness and depression, but we also know that we will get through it in the end. Whether it takes six months, a year, two years, or even more, there will come a day when we can think back on the furry companion we lost with fondness and joy for the time they've spent with us. We will never forget them; they will always live on in our hearts and memories. But whenever we think of them, the pain and sorrow will be replaced with joy and hope.

I trust that this book gave you the hope and courage you need to keep going. Even though the pain is still there, you can push through it to get to the other side and experience the joy of life again.

Please Submit Your Review Here

Appendix A:

Journaling Prompts

Journaling can be a great way to work through the emotions associated with pet loss grief. You can use these prompts to help you better understand your emotions and work through your pain.

Memories and Moments

- Describe your favorite memory with your pet. What made it so special?

- Write about a time when your pet comforted you. How did they make you feel better?

- List three things you miss most about your pet. Why are these memories significant?

Gratitude and Appreciation

- What are you most grateful for about having your pet in your life?

- Write a letter of thanks to your pet. What would you say to them if you could?

Expressing Emotions

- Describe the range of emotions you are feeling right now. How does each emotion manifest in your daily life?

- What are some of the hardest moments since your pet passed away? How did you cope with those times?

- Write about how your pet's passing has changed your daily routine and life.

Honoring Your Pet

- How do you plan to honor and remember your pet? Write about any rituals, memorials, or keepsakes you have or plan to create.

- If you could create a tribute to your pet, what would it be and why?

Reflection and Growth

- How has your pet influenced the person you are today?

- What lessons did you learn from your pet that you will carry forward in your life?

- Write about any changes in your perspective on life, love, and loss since your pet's passing.

Future Hopes and Healing

- What are your hopes for your healing journey? What steps can you take to help yourself heal?

- How can you use the love and lessons from your pet to bring positivity to your future?

Connecting with Others

- Write about conversations you've had with others about your pet. How have these interactions helped or hindered your grief process?

- Are there people in your life who understand your grief? How can you lean on them for support?

Daily Check-ins

- Each day, write down one thing that made you smile or feel a bit better, even if only for a moment.

- Track your emotional journey by writing about your feelings each day. Notice any patterns or changes over time.

Visualizing Peace

- Close your eyes and imagine a peaceful place where your pet is happy and at peace. Describe this place in detail.

- Visualize yourself in the future, feeling more at peace with your pet's passing. What does that future look like, and how do you get there?

Creative Expression

- Write a poem or a short story from your pet's perspective. What would they want to tell you?

- Create a list of songs, quotes, or pieces of art that remind you of your pet and explain why each one is meaningful to you.

Appendix B:

Pet Loss Support Resources

Coping with the grief of pet loss is never easy, but you don't have to go through it alone. Here are some resources you can turn to when you need help and support.

Online Support Groups and Forums

1. **Association for Pet Loss and Bereavement (APLB)**

   o Website: www.aplb.org

   o Offers online chat rooms and scheduled support group sessions.

2. **Rainbow Bridge**

   o Website: www.rainbowsbridge.com

   o Provides a Monday Candle Ceremony and forums where pet owners can share their grief and support each other.

3. **Pet Loss Support Page by Moira Anderson Allen**

   o Website: www.pet-loss.net

   o Features articles, support groups, and coping resources.

4. **Reddit - r/petloss**

   o Website: www.reddit.com/r/petloss/

   o An active community where members share their stories, offer support, and find comfort.

Counseling Services

1. **American Society for the Prevention of Cruelty to Animals (ASPCA) Pet Loss Hotline**

   o Hotline: (877) GRIEF-10 (877-474-3310)

   o Offers counseling and support for pet owners dealing with loss.

2. **Therapy Pet - Pet Loss Counseling**

   o Website: www.therapypet.org

   o Connects pet owners with counselors who specialize in pet loss.

Professional Associations and Organizations

1. **American Veterinary Medical Association (AVMA) - Pet Loss Support**

   o Website: www.avma.org/resources-tools/pet-owners/petcare/coping-loss-pet

   o Provides resources and support for pet owners dealing with loss.

2. **The Humane Society of the United States - Coping with Pet Loss**

   o Website: www.humanesociety.org/resources/how-cope-death-your-pet

   o Offers articles, support resources, and information on dealing with the death of a pet.

3. **International Association of Animal Hospice and Palliative Care (IAAHPC)**

   o Website: www.iaahpc.org

   o Provides resources for pet hospice care and support for pet loss.

Helplines and Hotlines

1. **Pet Loss Support Hotline by Cornell University College of Veterinary Medicine**

   o Hotline: (607) 253-3932

   o Offers phone support for grieving pet owners.

2. **Lap of Love Pet Loss Support Hotline**

   o Hotline: (855) 352-5683

   o Provides emotional support for those grieving the loss of a pet.

3. **Pet Compassion Careline**

   o Hotline: (855) 949-2273

   o Available 24/7 to offer support and comfort to grieving pet owners.

References

A quote by Anatole France. (n.d.). Good reads. Www.goodreads.com. https://www.goodreads.com/quotes/4432-until-one-has-loved-an-animal-a-part-of-one-s

Anderson, W. P., Reid, C. M., & Jennings, G. L. (1992). *Pet ownership and risk factors for cardiovascular disease.* NIH. *The Medical Journal of Australia,* *157*(5), 298–301. https://pubmed.ncbi.nlm.nih.gov/1435469/

AVMA. (n.d.). *Human-animal bond | American Veterinary Medical Association.* Www.avma.org. https://www.avma.org/resources-tools/one-health/human-animal-bond

Beetz, A., Uvnäs-Moberg, K., Julius, H., & Kotrschal, K. (2012). Psychosocial and Psychophysiological Effects of Human-Animal Interactions: The Possible Role of Oxytocin. *Frontiers in Psychology,* *3*(234). https://www.ncbi.nlm.nih.gov/pmc/articles/PMC3408111/

Behler, A. M. C., Green, J. D., & Joy-Gaba, J. (2020). "We Lost a Member of the Family": Predictors of the grief experience surrounding the loss of a pet. *Human-Animal Interaction Bulletin,* *2020.* https://doi.org/10.1079/hai.2020.0017

Bekoff, M. (2008). *The emotional lives of animals: a leading scientist explores animal joy, sorrow, and empathy - and why they matter.* New World Library.

Bennett, K. (2020, August 2). *How animals grieve.* Veterinary Teaching Hospital. https://vetmedbiosci.colostate.edu/vth/animal-health/how-animals-grieve/

Bradley University. (2018, August 24). *5 counseling strategies for loss and grief.* Bradley University Online.

https://onlinedegrees.bradley.edu/blog/counseling-strategies-for-loss-and-grief/

Brennan, D. (2021, June 11). *What to know about Oxytocin Hormone.* WebMD. https://www.webmd.com/sex-relationships/what-to-know-about-oxytocin

Children and grief by Age & Stage. (n.d.). Irish Childhood Bereavement Network. https://www.childhoodbereavement.ie/families/childrens-grief/

Cox, J. (2016, May 17). *How long does grief last? Timelines, symptoms, and getting help.* Psych Central. https://psychcentral.com/lib/grief-healing-and-the-one-to-two-year-myth/

Czajkowski, S. M., Arteaga, S. S., & Burg, M. M. (2022). Social support and cardiovascular disease. *Handbook of Cardiovascular Behavioral Medicine*, 605–630. https://doi.org/10.1007/978-0-387-85960-6_25

Dyring, L. (2022, October 23). *The surprisingly comforting science behind grief.* Inspire the Mind. https://www.inspirethemind.org/post/the-surprisingly-comforting-science-behind-grief

Field, N. P., Orsini, L., Gavish, R., & Packman, W. (2009). *Role of attachment in response to pet loss.* https://www.researchgate.net/publication/24279173_Role_of_Attachment_in_Response_to_Pet_Loss

Godfrey, H. (2022, November 1). *How long can a dog go without eating? A vet answers - Raised Right - Human-Grade Pet Food.* Raised Right Pets. https://www.raisedrightpets.com/blog/how-long-can-a-dog-go-without-eating/

Haude, K., McCarthy Veach, P., LeRoy, B., & Zierhut, H. (2016). Factors influencing the decision-making process and long-term interpersonal outcomes for parents who undergo preimplantation genetic diagnosis for Fanconi Anemia: a qualitative investigation. *Journal of Genetic Counseling, 26*(3), 640–655. https://doi.org/10.1007/s10897-016-0032-0

Healing your brain after loss: How grief rewires the brain. (2021, September 29). American Brain Foundation. https://www.americanbrainfoundation.org/how-tragedy-affects-the-brain/

How science has proven funerals help with the grieving process - Krause Funeral Home & Cremation Services. (2023, March 17). Krausefuneralhome.com. https://krausefuneralhome.com/blog/how-science-has-proven-funerals-help-with-the-grieving-process/

Jordan, J., & Neimeyer, R. (n.d.). *Does grief counseling work?* https://doi.org/10.1080/07481180390233362

Khalid, A., & Dildar, S. (2019). Effect of pet interaction on stress reduction and positive mood enhancement among pet-owners and non-owners. *Human-Animal Interaction Bulletin, 2019.* https://doi.org/10.1079/hai.2019.0005

King, B. J. (2014). *How animals grieve.* Univ Of Chicago Press, Chicago [Ill.

Koster, S. (2007). *Hachi-Ko.* Publishamerica Incorporated.

Kübler-Ross, E. (2014). *On death & dying: What the dying have to teach doctors, nurses, clergy & their own families.* Scribner, A Division Of Simon & Schuster, Inc. (Original work published 1969)

Michigan State University. (2018, December 7). *The human-animal bond throughout time.* The College of Veterinary Medicine at Michigan State University. https://cvm.msu.edu/news/perspectives-magazine/perspectives-fall-2018/the-human-animal-bond-throughout-time

Mitima-Verloop, H. B., Mooren, T. T. M., Kritikou, M. E., & Boelen, P. A. (2022). Restricted mourning: Impact of the COVID-19 pandemic on funeral services, grief rituals, and prolonged grief symptoms. *Frontiers in Psychiatry,* *13.* https://doi.org/10.3389/fpsyt.2022.878818

My dog died and my heart is broken: Hurt, hope, and healing. (2010, October 13). Psych Central. https://psychcentral.com/voices/when-pets-die-human-hearts-break

Pirrone, F., Albertini, M., Mazzola, S. M., Pierantoni, L., Bavagnoli, F., & Vigo, D. (2015). Correlation between the size of companion dogs and the profile of the owner: a cross-sectional study in ItalyMarian. *Dog Behavior,* *1*(2), 32–43. https://doi.org/10.4454/db.v1i2.14

Slavik, D. (n.d.). *Building a bond with your K9 partner.* Www.uspcak9.com. Retrieved July 3, 2024, from https://www.uspcak9.com/index.php?option=com_dailyplane tblog&view=entry&category=canine-training-articles&id=21:building-a-bond-with-your-k9-partner

Struck, K. (2021, June 30). *The rainbow bridge: Helping kids cope with the loss of a pet.* The Stepmom Project. https://www.thestepmomproject.com/rainbow-bridge/

Tartakovsky, M. (2022, May 13). *Mindfulness for anger: How it works and guided meditation.* Psych Central. https://psychcentral.com/blog/a-mindful-practice-to-fully-feel-your-anger

The five animals that grieve. (n.d.). HarperCollins Children's Books. https://www.harpercollins.com/blogs/harperkids/the-five-animals-that-grieve

Thomas, J., & Sours, T. (2007). Multiple lacerations of the heart: When grief accumulates. *Faculty Publications and Presentations.* https://digitalcommons.liberty.edu/ccfs_fac_pubs/15/

Trepany, C. (2023, October 21). *My dog died two months ago. Pet loss causes deep grief that our society ignores.* USA TODAY. https://www.usatoday.com/story/life/health-wellness/2023/10/31/pet-loss-disenfranchised-grief/71375731007/#

Viswesvaran, C., Sanchez, J. I., & Fisher, J. (1999). *The role of social support in the process of work stress: A meta-analysis. Journal of Vocational Behavior,* *54*(2), 314–334. https://doi.org/10.1006/jvbe.1998.1661

Watson, S. (2023, June 13). *Oxytocin: The love hormone.* Harvard Health. https://www.health.harvard.edu/mind-and-mood/oxytocin-the-love-hormone

Please Submit Your Review Here

Made in the USA
Columbia, SC
26 September 2024